VIRTUES WORK

Soar at Work. Soar at Life.
Here's How.

Alexander Cummings

Clovercroft Publishing

Virtues Work

©2020 by Alexander Cummings

Published by Clovercroft Publishing, Franklin, Tennessee

Edited by Lee Titus Elliott

Cover and Interior Design by Suzanne Lawing

Printed in the United States of America

978-1-948484-92-3

info@virtueswork.com

This book is dedicated with thanks and gratitude to those in my family who have been models of the virtues of patience, good counsel, encouragement, and love throughout this project—particularly Paula, Ian, & Sophie.

Contents

"Whenever we find a good human act,
it must correspond to some human virtue."

St. Thomas Aquinas,
Summa Theologica, 1265–1274

The Virtues: Marvels within Your Grasp

The list of life's certainties is short: the sun rises in the east and sets in the west; tomorrow is another day; death and taxes, of course; and a few more. You can add another to the list: you can't go wrong using the virtues.

The virtues have been helping people for millennia. Plato and Aristotle were among the first to write extensively about the virtues. The virtues take what is good within us, refine it, strengthen it, and bring it into play in all sorts of situations throughout life. This is how the virtues transform people and lives. By using the virtues, people build on that good and become happier and more admirable and models and promoters of what is good.

The virtues do this in your personal life and your relationships, and they can do this while you work. The virtues are life's wonders, and they can be work's wonders. No matter what kind of work you do—paid or volunteer—or where you are in your career—just starting or nearing retirement—the virtues can transform the time you spend at work, turning it into a source of meaning, pride, and joy.

But many people don't consider these marvels while they work. For various reasons, they're reluctant to use the virtues while they work, or it doesn't even occur to them that they can use them at work.

This book introduces you to the virtues: what they are, what they can do for you, and how to use them. And, most significantly, this book adapts the seven most important virtues for use while you work. The virtues can be of great benefit to you at work, and, with these adaptations, the virtues you hear about on Sunday can be used easily on Monday.

> The more we use the virtues, the happier life is.

You reap tremendous rewards from using the virtues in daily life and at work—both personal and professional rewards. Your life will be even happier, your relationships deeper, and your character more admired. At work, the virtues give you more skills you can apply to your work—leading to greater success—and they give your work greater meaning: you know that your work makes a difference.

I wrote this book because, like you, I have been given the immense gift of the virtues by God. But, like you, I haven't taken the gift fully out of the box—too often I leave the virtues and all of their promises wrapped and unused. That's a self-inflicted wound; the more we actually use the virtues, the happier life is. Too many people ignore this gift or don't understand it. Some people even have an aversion to this gift. In this book, I explain this gift clearly and show you how to apply the virtues, one at a time, easily and naturally. I focus particular attention on applying the virtues to work, an area where they don't get enough thought. Work doesn't have to be troublesome or a necessary evil. It's really an opportunity—a largely overlooked opportunity—to use the virtues and lay the foundation for a better life.

My work as a consultant to large financial services firms helped shape this book. Part of my work involved developing corporate-values programs for clients and communicating the values to their employees. Unfortunately, I saw that noble ideals etched in marble in the lobby or incorporated into directives, incentives, or workshops just didn't instill values into employees. CEOs can't make their employees honest or caring. Those virtues actually come from the bottom up; employees have to decide for themselves whether to use these virtues and learn how to make them second nature. Corporate values programs don't do this. But this book does. It shows you the ideals worth adopting, why they're worth adopting, and how to make them yours.

The Book You're Holding

This book was written to be used, not to sit on a shelf. That's why it's short, not long and ponderous. It's clear, concise, and easy to read. It's structured to be a quick reference; the important points, definitions, and helpful techniques are easy to find and refer to.

The book is clearly organized:

- Chapters 1 through 4 explain what the virtues are and what they can do for you.

- Chapter 5 details the seven most important virtues. It defines them and spells out how you can use them—and what happens if you don't.

- Chapter 6 walks you through four steps that will enable you to make the life-changing virtues second nature. The heart of this part is the Program. It's easy to implement and helps you take any of your current habits that fall short and replace them with the virtues, enabling you to soar at work and in life.

The book is also full of classic anecdotes. The virtues are timeless, and stories of past leaders using the virtues remain valuable and instructive. These anecdotes give you clear examples of the many and varied opportunities to use the virtues while you work. After reading this book, you'll recognize and be able to capitalize on those opportunities when they pop up. You'll also learn from the folly of others; a few of the anecdotes are about prominent people who ignored these virtue opportunities and slipped into behaviors that eventually hurt their careers.

The virtues are powerful engines of good waiting to move you to the ideal place you want to go. Sure, the virtues can get you closer to that ideal place if you only use them outside of work. But why do that? That limits them...and you: it only opens the gift part way. Open the gift all the way. Work is full of opportunities to use the virtues. Using them there speeds you on your way to replacing imperfect behaviors, allowing you to flourish in the workplace and outside of it.

Finally, when you take advantage of those opportunities at work, you'll see your work in a new light. You'll view work as giving you a chance to soar as a person. Work will become a place to experiment with the virtues and grow—a laboratory whose fruits are greater happiness, peace, and success.

1.

Life's Accessible Wonders

Every so often, you meet people whose behavior you truly admire. You see them in action, and you are impressed by their kindness or wisdom or strength of character. You and everyone else are attracted by the qualities these people radiate. They make you want to be better, to be like them. How do they do it? And what separates them from so many others?

They use the virtues.

The virtues are a wonder. They're one of God's greatest gifts to humanity. They will be defined in detail later in the book. For now, know that when used habitually, the virtues lead to all that is good—happiness, a sterling character, the admiration of others, a sense of fulfillment.

You've certainly noticed that there is much more going on at work than work. People find opportunities to do all kinds of things, like socializing, dating, paying their bills, and using social media. But the most important "nonwork" opportunity is often overlooked, even though it can have a greater impact on you than almost anything in your life, including your work. The most important "nonwork" opportunity is that work gives you a chance to use the virtues. This is good news. It means that all of the good, the wisdom, and the happiness that the virtues bring to life are yours, if you use the virtues while you work.

> All human activity gives you an opportunity to use the virtues.

And this is true of any kind of work: paid work, volunteer work, the work of a student, the work of a parent. All work—in fact, all human activity—gives you an opportunity to use the virtues.

Most often people think of the virtues outside of the workplace—for example, the compassion shown by the Good Samaritan while traveling or the courage of someone who saves a stranger from an attack. But the virtues have a role in all human endeavors. And work is a big endeavor.

The hours you spend at work shape who you are, just as the time spent with friends or your spouse and family shapes who you are. Use the virtues while you work, and you'll see their power for positive change flowing into every part of your life. You'll reap their rewards and become one of those people who are widely admired. Read this anecdote for a noteworthy example of the positive power of a virtue at work after a dark, dark day.

> The virtues lead to all that is good.

Jimmy Dunne and 9/11

On September 11, 2001, Jimmy Dunne worked for a medium-sized investment banking firm. He and two other executives were the committee that ran the firm. That day Dunne was playing golf with clients, instead of working at the company's World Trade Center headquarters. Sixty-six of the firm's eighty-three World Trade Center employees were killed that day—including the two other executives who ran the company. In total, more than one-third of the whole firm died on September 11. The firm faced extreme financial difficulties after the attack, and Dunne struggled to keep the firm open. In spite of the difficulties, Dunne decided to continue paying the salaries of all those who had been killed. He paid them until the end of 2001, and then he paid their bonuses, making sure that year's bonus equaled or exceeded the highest bonus ever received by those employees. He made sure any commissions on accounts opened before September 11 went to the victim's family until the end of the year, rather than to the firm or the person who now managed the account. He also pledged that the firm would pay the cost of health insurance for all victims' survivors for years. This is the virtue of compassion used at work under extraordinarily difficult circumstances.

Virtues Work

This book does two things: it explains how to use the virtues in all areas of life, and it adapts the virtues for use in today's workplace. Even though the virtues belong at work, work is different from life outside of work. The virtues must be used in a different way than they can be used in other areas of your life, because you have different responsibilities and constraints at work than you do outside of work. When adapted, the virtues fit seamlessly, naturally, and quietly into your work.

Some people are reluctant to use the virtues or don't think the virtues belong at work. This usually comes from misunderstanding the virtues. This book tackles these misunderstandings head-on, opening everyone in the workplace to the virtues. It defines the virtues and uses practical, concrete steps to teach you how to use them and, specifically, how to use them while you work. The book features historical, inspiring anecdotes of business leaders using the virtues—or failing to use them—to help you identify opportunities for using the virtues at work. It also makes clear what happens to you if you don't use the virtues; in other words, how every virtue saves you from the failings that keep you from the good things in life. Finally, this book introduces the

> The virtues fit seamlessly, naturally, and quietly into your work.

Program, a straightforward, step-by-step guide to making the virtues your new habits. It's not difficult or time-consuming, but it will be life-altering, in the best sense. The virtues build on your strengths and overpower your weaknesses, making you a person that others admire and emulate.

2.

Good Things Happen When the Virtues Are Habits

The virtues can make your life—no matter how wonderful it is—better. Your positive qualities can be more numerous and more visible to all. And you can be more successful at work and find your work more satisfying. The virtues are powerful enough to do all of that, and they're at your call. Here's what the virtues will enable you to do:

Soar as a person

You have qualities and potential that haven't been fully tapped. When the virtues are habits, these God-given gifts will be used more fully and openly. And when that happens, what is great in you will shine; you'll be admired and be an example for others. You'll have a sterling, unshakable character and be even happier, making those around you happier. Here's an example of how this happens. When the virtue of justice is a habit, you'll treat everyone equitably. You'll be known to be absolutely just or fair, so you'll be widely respected. People will look to you for answers to tough problems, and your reputation will be unimpeachable.

Have more success at work

Many are skeptical that using the virtues leads to greater success at work, but it's true. Business school professors agree. Professor Jeffery Sonnenfeld at Yale University's business school, an expert on leadership, has identified five elements that make an effective leader, and four of them tie directly into the virtues.[1] Jim Collins, formerly of the Stanford Graduate School of Business and author of

> Of the five traits great managers share, all of them come from the virtues.

the best-selling management book *Good to Great,* sees several virtues, particularly humility, as vital in helping managers outperform their competitors. In addition, the Gallup organization's researchers have identified five traits that great managers share, and all of them come from the virtues.[2]

More success comes about because, in addition to being important in itself, every important virtue—particularly the ones discussed in this book—helps develop some of the skills that lead to success. You become skilled at something necessary for success as a byproduct of using a virtue. For example, as the virtue of prudence becomes a habit, you develop extraordinarily good judgement.

The skills the virtues give you are both strategic skills and soft skills—the skills that help you see the big picture and those that help you interact with people in a better, more effective way. For example, using the virtue of compassion helps you effortlessly strengthen your relationships with colleagues and clients. Or as you use the virtue of hope, you inspire those around you and motivate them to succeed.

Find more fulfillment from work

The virtues free you from something that is all too common—the feeling that your work doesn't matter, that you're simply a drone showing up every day to repeat the same tasks. The virtues bring meaning and fulfillment to your work; they show you its importance and bring enthusiasm and interest back to work.

Here's the key: using the virtues completely causes you to focus on others and not on yourself. So the focus of your work becomes other people, or a cause, not yourself. And this gives your work meaning. As Leo Tolstoy wrote, "Man finds happiness only in serving others." That's our God-given nature. You can see this effect in soldiers or members of an athletic team; their efforts have meaning and importance to them primarily when their efforts are focused on something outside of themselves. Jim Collins's research shows that service—working for something outside of yourself—is an essential ingredient in successful and *meaningful* work. Jimmy Dunne's work certainly had more meaning after 9/11, since he knew that his work helped the victims' families. And the virtues will do that for you in your work. Particularly helpful in adding meaning to your work is the virtue of self-control; it helps you focus on something other than yourself, and it enables you to rise above doing only what you feel like doing so that you can help others.

Live with integrity

You have integrity when the principles you say you live by and your actions are the same. The virtues spell out a clear code of superior conduct. And when you make the virtues your habits, you live by that code; you have integrity. People see this and admire it greatly. "In business, ethics and integrity are the bedrock upon which careers are built,"[3] the former head of accounting giant Deloitte says. And integrity becomes increas-

> People notice those who do good.

ingly important as you advance at work, and your actions have consequences for your entire organization. One virtue that helps you in particular to live with integrity is courage. When you're courageous, you live by your superior code, even if there might be a negative consequence to doing so.

Think clearly

Wishful thinking, muddled reasoning, or ignoring bad news can ruin a career or an organization, while clear thinking is invaluable to success. Using the virtues requires you to apply your reason to everything happening around you. Could there be a better way to be a clear, incisive thinker than to use reason to examine reality? One virtue, in particular, strengthens your ability to think clearly, the virtue of humility. It requires you to look at yourself and your circumstances as they really are and act accordingly.

As you use the virtues at work, good things will happen to you. And others will be inspired by your example. People know what is good. They would usually like to do it, but they are often distracted or hesitant. But they notice those who do good. And they're motivated to follow their good example.

As you think about all there is to gain personally

and professionally from using the virtues at work, your thoughts about your time at work will change. Work will never be nonstop fun, but its hidden, positive aspects will become clearer. It is an opportunity given to you by God, in part, to develop and use the virtues. Tremendous rewards will come to you, as you use the virtues, making the opportunity to grow in the virtues the most valuable part of your work.

Finally, there's one more reason to use the virtues at work. You and your life are important, and it is up to you to make your life as wonderful as it can be. Who you are as a person shapes your relationships, the kind of life you have, and, ultimately, your happiness. You spend a lot of time at work, and your actions there set the pattern for how you act outside of work. When you use the virtues at work, you are leveraging that time to become a more outwardly focused person and a person who uses his or her interior strengths to their utmost. As a result, who you are as a person changes, producing deeper relationships and lasting happiness, which are true success and meaning in life.

3.

The Virtues

The virtues are a powerful force for good in your life because they're a particular kind of habit. Any of your actions can become a habit through repetition. But not all actions, and not all habits, are good. Good habits shape you, your character, and your life in a positive way; bad ones don't. And the virtues are the best habits you can develop. As the English poet John Dryden wrote, "We first make our habits, then our habits make us." Change your habits, and you change yourself.

Work Habits Don't Stay at Work

Logically, Dryden's observation applies to your actions and habits at work, too. How you repeatedly act at work forms habits that shape who you are and your life at work and outside of work. Simply put, the kind of person you are at work is the kind of person you are outside of work. This happens because you spend much of your time at work—more than half of your waking hours for a full-time job. And work increasingly spills over into home life, as more people work from home or bring work home or on vacation. Two-thirds of employees check in with the office on the weekend,[4] and 42 percent of employees feel "compelled" to contact work while on vacation.[5] With work's huge presence in your life, the habits you form at work become your habits outside of work—good or bad. Fortunately, work provides ample opportunities—big and small, open and hidden—to build outstanding habits—in other words, the virtues. Consider the example of John D. Rockefeller:

John D. Rockefeller In Control

When John D. Rockefeller ran Standard Oil in the late nineteenth century, a top executive made an error that cost the company $2 million. One of Rockefeller's business partners went into Rockefeller's office, expecting to hear a long tirade about the error and its cost from the meticulous, precise oilman. Instead, Rockefeller was writing peacefully at his desk. He said that, before talking to the executive who had made the error, he wanted to make a few notes. He showed what he was writing to his business partner. The notes were titled "Points in Favor" and listed the qualities of the man

> The kind of person you are at work is the kind of person you are outside of work.

who had made the error and the decisions he had made that had earned Standard Oil much more than $2 million.

Rockefeller reacted to this error with justice and self-control—two of the virtues. They turned an ordinary event at work into an ennobling incident, shaping everyone for the better.

The Virtues—Defined

C. S. Lewis writes, in *Mere Christianity,* that there are some behaviors or habits that are universally seen as good. These are acknowledged by everyone to be characteristic of outstanding people and outstanding lives. The most significant of these habits are the virtues. **A virtue is a habit that develops the good within you.** In other words, the virtues strengthen your noble qualities—those that all people aspire to and are the fulfillment of human nature's potential. The virtues produce outstanding people and outstanding lives.

The virtues do such tremendous good because they take the greatest gifts given to us—our reason and will—and use them in the way they were intended to be used—that is, focused on somebody or something outside of oneself and not in a self-interested way. Work is an ideal place to develop the virtues because it brings you into contact with a mix of people and their needs, and it calls on many of your talents and abilities. And the virtues you develop at work are yours, your habits—you take them with you, as your career and your life change.

Great thinkers throughout history—Plato, Aristotle, St. Augustine, St. Thomas Aquinas—saw the importance of the virtues. Benjamin Franklin wrote about and practiced the virtues. These thinkers were focused on our goal in life, so they wanted to find the key to a successful, happy life. They differed in their conceptions of a suc-

> Benjamin Franklin wrote about and practiced the virtues.

cessful life, but they all believed the virtues were the best way to achieve one. Nicholas Dreystadt, a 20th century business executive, demonstrated what some of these great thinkers had in mind.

Nicholas Dreystadt Changes Cadillac

Nicholas Dreystadt came to America at age thirteen. He came as an apprentice to a Mercedes auto-racing team. When he got older, he worked for General Motors, in its Cadillac division. At that time, the late 1920s and early 1930s, General Motors had as a corporate policy that it wouldn't sell Cadillacs to black people; General Motors believed that such a policy would maintain Cadillac's exclusive image.

Dreystadt travelled around the country for Cadillac, and he knew there was demand for Cadillacs in the black community. Black people were barred from many of the traditional ways of conveying success or status, such as living in exclusive neighborhoods or belonging to clubs, for example. But owning a Cadillac was a status symbol that could be had, if one circumvented General Motors' policy. So many prominent black people paid white people to purchase Cadillacs for them.

Cadillac's sales plummeted in the early part of the Great Depression, and, in 1932, General Motors' Board of Directors met to decide whether they should close money-losing Cadillac. Dreystadt knocked on the door of the room where the Board of Directors was meeting and asked to address the Board and General Motors' legendary president, Alfred P. Sloan. This was highly unusual for a midlevel employee. He was given ten minutes. He told them they could increase sales and save Cadillac by selling cars to black people. Nicholas Dreystadt was bringing the virtue of justice to work.

The Board considered Dreystadt's proposal and accepted it—up to a point. The Board gave Cadillac's management permission to sell to black people, but it gave management only eighteen months to restore profitability; if profitability hadn't been restored at the end of the trial period, Cadillac would be closed.

Two years after the Board meeting and with the country still deep in the Depression, sales of Cadillacs were up by 70 percent, and Cadillac was breaking even. The Board promoted Dreystadt to president of the Cadillac division, which he soon turned into General Motors' most profitable division.

The Seven Key Virtues

There are many virtues, and some are more important than others. Seven are particularly significant, and these are the virtues you'll find most beneficial. Using a framework influenced by St. Thomas Aquinas's writings and modified for the workplace, these are the seven vital virtues and the primary quality each virtue produces:

1. **Compassion**, which leads to kindness.

2. **Justice**, which leads to fairness.

3. **Prudence**, which leads to wisdom.

4. **Courage**, which leads to bravery.

5. **Self-control**, which leads to maturity.

6. **Humility**, which leads to honesty with yourself.

7. **Hope**, which leads to a positive approach and motivation.

Compassion and justice govern your interactions with people. They change how you treat others, which affects your relationships and how others perceive you. The other virtues—prudence, courage, self-control, humility and hope—do most of their work within you.

They change how you make decisions and why you act; when you use them, you're driven by your reason and will to do the right thing, rather than by whim or pure emotion, which may not lead to what's right.

These seven virtues are the foundation of all good behavior. Every other good habit you have comes from them. Your important good habits (such as honesty and patience, which are products of justice and courage) and less-significant habits (such as friendliness, which comes from compassion) all flow from these seven virtues. Adopting the seven key virtues will improve all your actions in and out of work quickly and easily.

Quickly and easily? Yes. Using the virtues isn't time-consuming. In general, they will simply modify your current behavior. You don't necessarily add anything to your life; as opportunities to use a virtue arise, use your new habit rather than your old one. Simply substitute new, positive habits for older, less-good ones. Soon you'll notice the positive effects of the virtues infiltrating all aspects of your life.

You certainly use the virtues already while you work and often without thinking about it. But probably not as frequently as you could. The virtues should guide you every time you interact with someone or every time you're getting ready to act. This is not as hard as it seems. The Program in this book eases you into making the virtues habits one step at a time and one virtue at a time. The key is how often you use the virtue; the more often, the faster the virtue becomes second nature for you. And any use of the virtues—big or little—contributes to establishing them as your new habits.

Interestingly, you're not alone in valuing the virtues and putting them into practice while you work. Many organizations—including large multinational corporations—have responded to their workers' desire to make their work meaningful and to lead richer, integrated lives by helping workers look at themselves and their behavior. These organizations offer training to help workers better themselves as individuals, and some go further, employing people dedicated to helping workers assess and improve themselves. The time you spend at work plays a significant part in shaping what kind of person you become, and workers are asking for, and getting, more opportunities to focus on this while at work.

> The Program in this book eases you into making the virtues habits.

4.

What If You Don't Use the Virtues?

Take this anecdote as a warning. John Henry Patterson is an example of what happens if you don't make the seven key virtues your habits: you'll fall into self-destructive behavior. In other words, behavior that undermines the good you're trying to accomplish, personally and professionally.

John Henry Patterson Goes Too Far

John Henry Patterson was a sales-and-business genius who founded what became office-equipment maker NCR. He failed to use the virtue of justice in his focus on his employees' health, and that failure led him to a self-destructive extreme. To determine how healthy NCR employees were, Patterson had all NCR employees weighed and measured every six months. Then he dictated the foods they could eat: he banned coffee, tea, bread and butter, and salt and pepper, and he demanded that employees eat shredded wheat and malted milk. Patterson even fired an employee because he didn't approve of the way the employee ate his soup. Many NCR employees bristled at how Patterson treated them and quit or were fired when they refused to follow Patterson's practices. The steady flow of well-trained ex-NCR employees to NCR's competitors drained Patterson's company of talent and put it at a disadvantage.

Self-Destructive Behavior

Self-destructive is a strong term, but acting in a self-destructive way is what happens when you don't use the virtues. How? In any situation, you have a range of behaviors open to you—some good, like the virtues, and some bad. When you choose not to use a virtue, you're choosing a less-good behavior or even a bad behavior. When these choices are repeated, these behaviors will become habits, which makes it harder to use the virtues and moves you away from the personal and professional rewards you receive from using the vir-

> Character flaws drive people away.

tues. This runs counter to your ultimate goals; it is self-destructive. For example, Patterson chose to act in an unjust way that wound up alienating his employees and strengthening his competitors—a self-destructive act for a businessman. Interestingly, Aristotle pointed out that a virtue—the right behavior—sits between two opposing self-destructive behaviors in the range of behaviors you can choose from. For example, the virtue of courage sits between cowardice and recklessness, two self-destructive behaviors.

This isn't theoretical. You almost certainly have some of these self-destructive habits now. They might not dominate your behavior yet, but they're grappling with constructive, positive habits for dominance. Human nature being what it is, if you're not tapping the power of the virtues and you're not trying to improve, you'll make self-destructive choices and slide away from the habits that make life better. And the further you slide away from the virtues, the harder it is to start using them. The virtues help you avoid self-destructive choices, no matter how tempting they might be.

For the Hesitant

For some people, the idea of using the virtues while they work is new, and they may be hesitant, but they shouldn't hold themselves back. Reluctance to use the virtues at work often comes from being unaware of the positive power of the virtues or from a misunderstanding about the virtues. When examined, reluctance doesn't make sense. Consider these common reasons for turning away from the virtues:

Less Competitive?—Some believe the virtues, especially compassion, will make them less competitive, or naïve. The opposite is true. As you read in Chapter 2, using the virtues makes you a clear thinker and mentally sharper. The virtues are built on the gift of reason: reasoning about your situation, weighing inputs and circumstances, and then acting. Users of the virtues are less likely to be duped by shady characters or illogical thinking than others.

Too Nice?—Some imagine the virtues will make them "too nice" for work or wishy-washy. But all the virtues require you to use your will to put them into practice. Exercising your will leads to firmness of character, drive, and mental toughness, which help you rather than hindering you at work.

Workplace Disapproval?—Perhaps you work in an organization that you fear may be hostile to the virtues and that using them will get you in trouble. Every organization values some of the virtues, but it may not recognize them as virtues. If compassion or justice is frowned upon at your organization, maybe courage or prudence is admired. Work on the virtues your employer approves of first; then move on quietly to using the other virtues.

(As an aside, ask yourself if you really want to work

in an organization that shuns many of the virtues. Working at such an organization is harming you—being immersed in its atmosphere does nothing positive for you as a person. And this kind of an organization is acting self-destructively. As John Pepper, former Chairman and CEO of Procter & Gamble, said: "Values are fundamental to retaining the kind of employees a firm… need[s] to succeed.")

Compartmentalization?—Or, finally, some people reach a compromise with themselves—consciously or unconsciously: they will use the virtues outside of work but not at work; they will "compartmentalize"—act one way at work and a different way with family and friends. They plan to reserve certain behavior for work—being bossy, crude, or unsympathetic, for example—because of the type of job they have or the type of people they work with, and then drop this behavior when they leave work. But when actions are repeated, they become habits. And habits can't be turned off and on. How you act at work is basically how you'll act outside of work.

> Every organization values some of the virtues.

Bad habits tend to be effortless to acquire and use. It's part of our weakness as humans. We slide toward the selfish and the easy, particularly if those bad habits produce results we like, or results that are celebrated at work. Good habits, on the other hand, require something else—the desire to do good, and the will to repeat it until the habit is set. Since bad habits are easy to fall into, they're more likely to replace a good habit without the person noticing than vice versa. Trying to compartmentalize undermines the effort to turn back bad habits and establish good habits, the virtues.

Compartmentalizing, if it worked, would only allow the compartmentalizer to repeat behavior at work that wasn't good enough to use at home, to "dumb down" his or her behavior. How does that have a good long-term effect on anybody? How will that help anybody soar? Those who try to compartmentalize wind up paying a high price to attempt the impossible: they deny themselves the winning power of the virtues, and their bad habits will spread to life outside of work, bringing with them a multitude of negative consequences. Maybe not immediately, but they will in due time. And you'll find that bad habits are often tolerated or excused while a person is successful or in a position of power, but once a setback comes, the character flaws drive people away.

The virtues are a wonder. They are a gift freely available to you that can make you admired, a role model, a positive influence, and part of the solution to life's difficulties. They enhance every aspect of life, including work. The virtues transform work into a source of strength for you. And since Benjamin Franklin and other thinkers about the virtues focused on what makes for a successful, productive life, it comes as no surprise that the virtues will make you better and more fulfilled at your job. The next chapter of this book examines the seven key virtues and how to put them into practice and reap their bountiful rewards. All it requires is the desire to do so and a conscious decision to use the virtues—the decision to grow and soar.

5.

How to Use the Virtues

The virtues are universally admired, but that doesn't mean they're universally understood. Misconceptions and false notions have built up around the virtues, causing some people to avoid using them or, as was mentioned earlier, to assume they're inappropriate for the workplace. In contrast, a variety of wise people throughout history have determined that the virtues are the key to a successful life. Armed with the information in this chapter, you'll be able to use these marvels while you work and to take your life to a new level.

In this chapter, you'll examine the seven key virtues and discover the benefits of using them. You'll learn the definition of each virtue and get specific suggestions about how to use that virtue. You will also find, for each virtue, an easy way to determine whether you're using the virtue and, crucially, what happens to you if you don't use that virtue.

"Contrary to the old cliché, genuinely nice guys most often finish first or very near it."

MALCOLM FORBES,
AMERICAN PUBLISHER, BUSINESSMAN

Compassion, Which Leads to Kindness

Compassion profoundly affects your relations with other people. It's one of two key virtues whose activity is felt primarily outside of you, focused on others. People notice compassion and are impressed by it, especially at work, where it tends to be absent. Since you're judged by how you treat people, compassion has a significant impact on those who use it, as well as on those who receive it.

When Do You Use Compassion?

Any time someone asks you for a favor, you can use compassion. Or you can use it when you see that someone needs help, or when you think of something nice to do for someone. Compassion is all about focusing on other people and their needs, and opportunities to do that can come up at any time.

Working Definition of Compassion

Compassion is acting to relieve the needs of others.

When you use compassion, you pay attention to the needs of others—expressed and unexpressed—and you are ready to help, if you can.

But you shouldn't always help. Let your mind guide your heart. Your reason plays an active role when you use the virtue of compassion, as it does with all the virtues. Your decision to help must be determined by your reason, not only by your emotions. You may have obligations that can make helping someone a mistake, or there may be circumstances that can make helping someone the wrong decision. Your reason figures all of that out. If emotion alone is driving your response, it's easy to do too much or too little for someone. Reason allows you to use compassion without becoming soft or making you less competitive—so you can use compassion at work with no negative consequences.

Example of Compassion at Work— W. K. Kellogg

You can use compassion at work, even in organizations that face stiff competition. Will Keith Kellogg started his cereal business in his older brother's kitchen; the two of them had developed a new breakfast food for his brother's health care facility. It proved to be popular with the patients, so Will Keith Kellogg started selling it to the general population. By the 1920s, Kellogg's and rival Post Cereals were the largest cereal companies in America. Competition in the industry was tough, but Kellogg "regarded his workers as family and treated them accordingly."[7] For example, in contrast to most companies of the time that required their employees to work six days a week and ten or more hours a day, "Kellogg's [was] one of the first companies to institute the eight-hour day and try out the five-day week."[8] Kellogg also opened a nursery for mothers working at the company, and he had medical and dental clinics and a dietician to watch over the children's health.

In 1929, the Great Depression hit. Unemployment reached 25 percent, economic activity in the United States (GDP) fell by 30 percent, bread lines formed, and shanty towns sprang up. The suffering and human need were enormous. What could Kellogg, or any person, do to help?

> Reason allows you to use compassion without becoming soft.

Kellogg decided to hire more people. He already had three shifts working twenty-four hours a day making cereal. Still, Kellogg hired more people, but he had everybody work fewer than eight hours a day. He switched from three eight-hour shifts to four six-hour shifts; that way he could add an entire shift of workers. But, to prevent his current workers from losing money by working only six hours per day rather than eight, Kellogg raised everyone's per-hour pay.

Kellogg had an additional reason for cutting workers' hours; he had long dreamed of giving his workers a shorter workday in order to give them "better living and working conditions."[9] The Depression gave Kellogg his opportunity to act on this compassionate vision.

Workers responded to Kellogg's compassion. His cereal company soon had the highest worker productivity in the industry and extraordinary worker loyalty. By the end of the Depression, Kellogg's had passed Post Cereals to become the largest cereal company in the country.

Kellogg couldn't end the Depression, but he didn't let that stop him from using compassion. Nor did he get overwhelmed by the size of the problem. He determined what he could do to relieve people's needs, and he did it. And what he did was significant for those he was able to help.

How to Use Compassion

To use compassion, you need to ask yourself two questions. When you're asked for help, or when you see a person with a need, ask yourself, "Can I help?" and "Should I help?"

That second question brings your reason into play. It gets you to balance your desire to help with your responsibilities and obligations. And it can prevent you from offering help that could ultimately make the situation worse. If you decide against helping, take a moment to double-check your intentions; is your reason directing you, or is something self-destructive—laziness, self-centeredness—really guiding you?

Compassion On the Job...and Off

Compassion day-to-day doesn't usually call for actions as dramatic as Kellogg's. But even when you focus on meeting other people's small needs—when reason tells you that you should—everyone benefits, and you strengthen your habit of compassion. Day-to-day examples of compassion include the following:

- When you see someone, ask how the person is and ask about his or her interests, sincerely.

- Find someone who has too much to do and ask if you can help.

- Think of a person who treats you well, and try to treat everyone that way.

- Lend a hand—even when unasked—to those grappling with something large or unpleasant. Many people are reluctant to help if a task seems big or if they think they can't finish it. But all help is valued.

- Reach out to someone who has drifted away, because nobody likes to be forgotten.

- If you honestly think helping would make a situation worse, turn the person down gently when you are asked for help.

The hallmark of compassion is caring about others. You do them a favor or give them a hand, not because it's always easy—or even because you want to—but because you see someone who needs help. But you're not a soft touch; you balance helping with your obligations. And you don't help if you think it's going to do more harm than good. But your kind manner and openness soften the blow when you decide not to help.

Not Using Compassion— The Self-Destructive Habits

When you use compassion, you prevent yourself from slipping into habits that will ultimately be self-destructive. Compassion, like every virtue, is positioned between behaviors that ultimately bring hardship and unhappiness. In the moment, these behaviors can be explained away and are tempting, but they eventually make you self-absorbed and unreasonable. Compassion keeps you from the following:

Self-centeredness. Here, your focus is on yourself, not on others. Your needs and your wants are your primary concern. You can help others, but you choose not to. This behavior is unpleasant at work, and it's fatal to healthy personal relationships. Those who are self-centered can become cold, impersonal, uncaring, and unable to empathize with others. Will self-centeredness really help you soar or succeed?

Irresponsibility. Here, your responsibilities and obligations play second fiddle to the needs of others, even when your reason tells you otherwise. This causes your duties to go unfulfilled. You can't be counted on. In a misguided, often emotion-driven desire to help or be nice, you can fail those who count on you, or you can wind up being used.

Compassion Wins People Over

The key to a rich, full life is warm, strong long-term relationships. The strength of the bonds you form with people is largely determined by compassion. With the virtue of compassion, you put others and their needs before yourself. That selflessness creates a connection between you and those you help. The more frequently you use compassion while you work, the stronger the connections you establish between you and other people—colleagues, family, and friends.

Compassion Leads to Other Great Habits

Compassion has other habits related to it that also focus you on the needs of others. You'll find it easier to use these habits when you make the virtue of compassion a habit. Some of these additional habits are as follows:

✓ Forgiveness ✓ Generosity

✓ Benevolence ✓ Friendliness

"Justice is truth in action."

<small>BENJAMIN DISRAELI,
NINETEENTH-CENTURY PRIME MINISTER
OF GREAT BRITAIN</small>

Justice,
Which Leads to Fairness

Justice is a vital virtue for you to focus on. St. Thomas Aquinas wrote: "Justice is the most excellent of all the moral virtues." Justice has several traits that make it so important:

- It regulates your relations with other people—that is, it governs how you treat others.

- It's ubiquitous—every interaction you have with people can be either just or unjust: every interaction—not only at your work but also at your home.

- Justice is easy to assess—you have a sense of whether you are being treated fairly or not. So does everyone else.

- It's objective; therefore, people can see how fair you are and use that as a test of your character.

Since justice is apparent to everyone at work and outside of work, any progress made on justice will help you soar in everyone's eyes.

When Do You Use Justice?

With the virtue of justice, the goal is to be fair every time you interact with people. You can certainly use it when you're in charge, or when you're distributing something. But even if you aren't in charge, you can make sure that all the people you interact with get what they should: respect, a chance, an open mind, the fruits of their labor, and so on.

Working Definition of Justice

Justice, or fairness, is simply giving people their due— what they deserve, no more, no less. If you take more than you're due, you're acting unjustly, because that denies other people all they're due.

Your reason and your will have a role to play with justice, of course; you use your reason to determine what everyone is due, and you use your will to give it to each one of them—whether you feel like it or not, whether it's to your advantage or not.

It's important to note that the *virtue* of justice can be different from ways the terms "justice" or "fairness" are commonly used. Legal justice may not be just; an action may be legal even if it deprives some people what they're due. And the widespread idea of fairness as an equal outcome for all—everyone getting the same amount—isn't always just, either. For example, if one person on a team at work hasn't put in the same effort as others on the team, that person doesn't necessarily deserve a reward equal to that received by those who did most of the work.

Example of _Not_ Using Justice at Work— Steve Jobs

Every interaction with people is a chance to be just or unjust, as in the example of Nicolas Dreystadt of Cadillac (see Chapter 3). That was an excellent example of seeing and seizing an opportunity to use the virtue of justice at work. But what follows is an interaction in which the chance to be just was not seized.

In 1974, Steve Jobs was just back from a trip to India, the goal of which was to find himself. He was sick and had no money. He went back to his old job at Atari, a video and arcade game maker. At Atari, he volunteered to design the circuit board for a new game. For his work, Jobs would be paid a design fee of $700, and if his design used fewer computer chips than the number Atari engineers estimated would be necessary, Jobs would get a bonus of $100 for every chip saved.

> Wozniak never got the money he deserved.

Jobs had a problem. He couldn't design the circuit board; he didn't have the know-how or the skills. But his friend Steve Wozniak did have those. Wozniak designed calculators for Hewlett Packard, and Jobs convinced Wozniak to design Atari's circuit board in exchange for half of the $700 fee and all the video games Wozniak could play. Wozniak designed the new board after work in four late-night sessions. The design was so efficient that it used fifty fewer chips than Atari's engineers had anticipated. When Jobs turned the circuit board in, Atari was stunned by the design. Atari paid Jobs the $700 design fee and a $5,000 bonus for chips not used. Jobs split the $700 fee with Wozniak, but he didn't tell him about the bonus. Jobs kept the entire $5,000. Wozniak never got the money he deserved and was deeply hurt when, years later, he learned what Jobs had done.

Jobs's injustice continued after he and Wozniak founded Apple Computer. He "hog[ged] the credit"[10] for others' work and fired "employees in angry tantrums."[11] Jobs's behavior became so bad that Apple's Board of Directors had to intervene to remove Jobs "from all managerial duties."[12] Finally, in 1985, Apple's board fired Jobs from the company he had founded.

How to Use Justice

Since every interaction with people is either just or unjust and since people are watching you, it's crucial to know how to make your actions just. To do this, put aside your interests in any situation and ask yourself, "Is everyone in this situation getting what he or she deserves?"

An honest answer to this question saves you from taking what others are due, even through some sort of rationalization or excuse. It's likely that Steve Jobs had a rationalization that sounded reasonable to him for keeping the entire bonus Atari paid him. People usually don't set out to be unjust or to cheat others, but self-interest—a focus on oneself rather than others, which is at odds with the virtues' call to place others first—can allow injustice to creep in and be rationalized away. As German philosopher Josef Pieper wrote, "Whoever looks only at himself…cannot be just." But the simplicity of the question above and its focus on others can keep anyone just.

Of course, even at work, justice goes beyond money. People can also deserve praise, recognition, promotion, a chance, constructive criticism, or even a rebuke. And we all deserve respect, a hearing, and our dignity.

Justice On the Job...and Off

It's easy to forget that justice is constantly on the line, even in routine interactions with people—even a genius like Steve Jobs can forget. On the day-to-day level, giving people what they deserve includes doing things such as the following:

- When you hear a rumor about somebody, don't jump to conclusions. Listen to both sides.

- When you talk about people, don't gossip or speculate about their motives.

- After a successful project, give all people involved credit for their part in the success.

- When making a decision, avoid playing favorites

with certain people—including yourself.

- If you see that some people aren't getting what they should, try to fix the problem for them.

- Think about what you truly deserve—money, promotion, benefits—and make sure you get them.

When you have a reputation for being just, you're widely trusted, because people know you act fairly and impartially. You insist that all people—including yourself—get what they're entitled to, but no more. You see to it that no one accepts more than what is fair or gives away what he or she deserves because of pressure or circumstances. You give all people their fair share of tangible rewards, but you also give them the respect, the attention, and the benefit of the doubt they deserve. People notice this and remember.

Not Using Justice—
The Self-Destructive Habits

Self-destructive behavior can easily become a habit, because bad habits require little effort to obtain; it's the good habits that require reason and will. When the virtue of justice is one of your habits, you're prevented, without even realizing it, from forming two self-destructive, life-impoverishing habits. Justice saves you from becoming a:

Cheat. You take more than you deserve. This short-changes others, and people know when they've been cheated. Unethical or dishonest behavior may give you a short-term benefit, but you pay for it by losing the trust, respect, and loyalty of your coworkers and family.

Pushover. When you routinely accept less than you deserve, you shortchange yourself. You're explicitly or implicitly agreeing to be taken advantage of. You won't use enough reason or will to stop it. Don't be surprised if people think of you as weak and lose respect for you. Occasionally, it may be better to accept less than what you're due as an act of compassion or prudence, but make it clear why you're accepting less than you deserve.

Justice Wins People Over

People can't really be just unless they value other people and have respect for them. The just don't use, demean, or treat others badly on purpose. When you treat your coworkers, friends, and family justly, they see the respect and regard you have for them. And they respond by treating you better and by having more respect for you.

Justice also eliminates some of the friction that can develop between people. When someone consistently doesn't get what he or she deserves, resentment or a low level of anger can easily start to fester and create tension. People know what is fair. Your coworkers know. Your spouse knows. Even little children have a strong sense of fairness. Making the virtue of justice a habit prevents these corrosive feelings from getting started.

Justice Leads to Other Great Habits

The virtue of justice has many offshoots—admirable habits that are an aspect of giving all people their due. You'll demonstrate these regularly when justice is a habit, and each one, ultimately, like justice, will bring you happiness and peace. Some of them are as follows:

✓ Honesty   ✓ Sportsmanship

✓ Impartiality   ✓ Gratitude

✓ Tolerance

"Chance fights ever on the side of the prudent."

Euripides,
Fifth-Century BC Athenian playwright

Prudence,
Which Leads to Wisdom

Prudence is one of several virtues that has most of its direct impact on you rather than on other people. Aristotle called prudence practical wisdom. It governs how you make decisions and what drives you to act. When you use prudence, you put reason and reality in charge of your decision making and give your emotions and wishful thinking a reduced role—if any. It helps you find the answer to two important questions: what should I do and how should I do it? Prudence is essential at work, but it also has a large role outside of work, where some of your life's trickier decisions are made.

When Do You Use Prudence?

Prudence helps you make decisions the right way. Therefore, use prudence every time you make a decision. With small, everyday decisions, the stakes may be low, but prudence helps you make the best decisions. And with more important decisions, the virtue of prudence is vital.

Working Definition of Prudence

Prudence is choosing the best path to a worthy goal. Note that choosing—deciding—is integral to prudence.

And what is a "worthy goal"? This is an important

part of the virtue of prudence. A worthy goal is one that is reasoned out, suits your circumstances, and has its focus outside of yourself. Carefully plotting the best way to steal an elderly woman's purse because you want her money is not prudence; it may be cunning or shrewd, but not prudent (and it's illegal). The worthy goal raises you and your decisions above cunning and other undesirable habits.

And what is the "best path"? The best path gets you to your goal—or close to your goal—while keeping potential problems to a minimum and not wasting your resources.

Example of Prudence at Work— Phil Anschutz

Prudence is widely misunderstood. It's not a delaying tactic, nor is it excessive caution. Prudence involves using your reason and making a decision; it shows you the right way and the right time to act. Sometimes the practical wisdom of prudence may indicate that caution is best, but, at other times, taking bold action is the prudent course. In fact, prudence is especially helpful in a crisis, as this story about Phil Anschutz demonstrates. In a crisis, it is easy to be indecisive or impulsive. Prudence forces you to reason your way to the best decision.

Phil Anschutz started working full-time in his family's fledgling oil-exploration business because his father didn't have enough money to send him to law school.

In 1967, Anschutz was drilling wells in Wyoming and looking for his first big strike. When his crew hit a gusher, Anschutz guessed it was a significant find and borrowed money to buy leases to drill on the land around the gusher. But then disaster struck.

A spark from a truck started a devastating fire at one of the wells. Burning oil was shooting out of control and hundreds of feet into the air. Anschutz tried to hire Red Adair, the legendary oil-fire fighter, but Adair refused. Anschutz didn't have enough money to pay him.

Phil Anschutz was deeply in debt, his most important asset was on fire, and he couldn't afford to put it out. "I tell you, I thought that was the end of me in business,"[13] Anschutz said later.

Anschutz decided that the fire had showed he had found a lot of oil. He went to his partner in the well and asked to buy a bigger stake in the well. The other man saw his oil going up in flames and was happy to sell.

Anschutz knew John Wayne was making a movie based on Red Adair's life, *Hellfighters*. Anschutz sold to the movie studio the rights to film Red Adair putting out a fire—*his* fire—for $100,000. Anschutz then used that money to pay Red Adair. So Adair put out the fire, John Wayne got his movie, and Anschutz got his oil well working and made a profit on the fire.

Anschutz moved beyond emotions to prudence; he used his reason to work out a solution to his problem and get closer to his goal. And he demonstrated two skills you acquire when you use the virtue of prudence: good judgment and decisiveness—skills that are invaluable at work, at home, and in a crisis.

How to Use Prudence

To use prudence, follow a three-step framework that taps into your reason and your will:

1. Gather information.

2. Analyze it, assessing possible paths and keeping your worthy goal in mind.

3. Pick the best path.

This three-step framework brings reason and reality into the decision-making process, keeping wishful thinking and pure emotion from having too much influence. And this framework makes use of your will because it forces you to choose—decide on—a path.

Prudence leads you to the best decision you can make under the circumstances, although it doesn't guarantee that what you decide will enable you to reach your worthy goal—life has too many unknowns for that. But knowing prudence is guiding you to the best decision available helps you overcome common obstacles to making a good decision—or any decision—for example, the unending desire for more information, your own insecurity, outside pressure, or your mood at the time.

Prudence On the Job...and Off

You constantly make decisions at work and out-side of work. The stakes are high for some decisions and low for most, but, either way, it's best if prudence guides you. Using prudence every day means the following:

- When you have a decision to make, get input and advice from others before you make up your mind, if you have the time.

- If you have a decision to make and not much time, resist the impulse to make a snap decision; reason the best you can with the information you have, and then decide.

- When someone pushes for a certain action, look beyond persuasive words and appeals to emo-tion. Think about what makes sense, given your worthy goal.

- When it falls to you to make a decision, be deci-sive; it may be hard, but leaders must be decisive.

- After you have made a decision, don't change your mind, unless circumstances have changed significantly.

As prudence guides you, you'll gain wisdom. As you habitually use prudence, you'll reason through problems the right way, and your judgment will get better. You'll be counted on by colleagues, family, and friends to think about problems clearly and make sound decisions. Many people struggle with decisions: they don't like making them, or they put them off and hide behind requests for more information. Not you. You'll be decisive, and your decisions will be well-thought-out and focused on your goals.

Not Using Prudence—
The Self-Destructive Habits

Prudence keeps you from two traps that are self-destructive over time. Both traps can be emotionally appealing and may offer short-term advantages, but they weaken your ability to think clearly and to lead others. They also result in a loss of respect and less success at work. Prudence helps you stay away from the following:

> Use prudence every time you make a decision.

Foolhardiness. Here, you make decisions without thinking them through—you make them quickly or impulsively, before gathering and analyzing information. Or you base them on shallow thinking, bias, or information that may not be important or relevant. And the consequences or likely results of your decisions aren't considered. You can't make decisions that will consistently benefit you, your work, and your family if you don't think things through.

Indecisiveness. In this case, you don't make decisions. Or you don't stick with the decisions you've made. This may be caused by fear, emotions that dominate reason, a lack of confidence in your reasoning, or a pattern of overanalyzing. Indecisiveness leaves you at the mercy of circumstances or of others. It leads to missed opportunities and makes it unlikely you'll reach your worthy goal.

Prudence Wins People Over

Since you don't live or work in isolation, the benefits from using the virtue of prudence ripple out from you to others. Over time, prudence brings you good judgment and makes you decisive in the face of uncertainty or challenges. So not only can you steer your career and life wisely, but you can also guide your coworkers and your friends and family through life's unknowns, saving them from missteps and earning their admiration and gratitude.

Prudence Leads to Other Great Habits

Prudence helps cultivate related habits that can play a role in decision making and can contribute to wisdom. Once the virtue of prudence is a habit, these other habits become easier to use, and each brings its own rewards. Some of these habits are as follows:

✓ Foresight   ✓ Creativity

✓ Flexibility   ✓ Discernment

✓ Curiosity

"Common experience shows how much rarer is moral courage than physical bravery."

CLARENCE DARROW,
NINETEENTH-CENTURY AMERICAN LAWYER

Courage,
Which Leads to Bravery

The virtue of courage is universally admired. Everyone, regardless of the time or culture, values bravery. People look up to the brave, in part because the brave do what all people know they should do, but don't—or don't do often enough.

Courage comes in two forms. Occasionally, physical courage is called for at work or at home. That's the type of courage that enables you to run into a burning building or to stare down a bad guy. More frequently, you're called on to use moral courage. This is the quality that helps you speak up, take a stand, or stay the course in the face of opposition. Both forms of courage enable you to soar in the eyes of others.

When Do You Use Courage?

You need courage every time you know you should do something but you don't want to do it because, deep down, you're scared of what might happen. Courage helps you do what you should. Everyone has fears— some big, some little. But, if, because of fear, you find you're hesitating to speak up, to confront your coworker or manager, to accept a new job, or to reach out to someone, courage can help.

Working Definition of Courage

Courage is taking a risk to do the right thing.

What is at risk varies. In every case, the risk is that something you value might be lost if you do what's right. But if you're courageous, you do it anyway. You don't seek out risk or difficulty, but you don't shrink from it, either. You know bad things could happen, but you believe that doing the right thing is more important.

And what is the "right thing" to do? It's what the other virtues tell you to do—especially prudence. Courage works closely with the other virtues and with your reason. Together, they guide you to do the right thing.

Reason plays an important part in courage, because many fears are irrational. Reason weakens fear. Fear is an emotion that can override your reason if you allow it to do so. Fear often exaggerates—far beyond reality—the chances of a bad outcome happening, or its consequences.

> Fear can wear many disguises.

The courageous aren't fearless. But courage lets them control their fears; therefore, their fears don't control them. It's human to have fears, but you can use your reason and your will to control or overcome them.

Example of Courage at Work—
William Milfred Batten

William Milfred Batten's job didn't require any physical courage, but it provided a perfect opportunity for moral courage. The stakes were high, and there is a particularly admirable aspect to Batten's story: nobody would have known if he had chickened out or played it safe. But that wouldn't have been the right thing to do.

Batten worked at J. C. Penney. He started as a shoe salesman in a Penney store in West Virginia shortly after college and worked his way up to become a vice president of the J. C. Penney Corporation. It was 1957, and J. C. Penney still used the same business model it started with when the company was founded in 1902. It saw the pillars of its success as its policies of accepting cash-only sales, placing stores mainly in small towns, and selling primarily soft goods (clothing). The company's founder—J. C. Penney, a legend in retailing—sat on the Board of Directors and was still active in the management of the company.

Batten was sure there was trouble ahead. He saw America, particularly retailing in America, changing after World War II. He thought J. C. Penney's style of selling would soon be obsolete. He was convinced the company had to make fundamental changes: he wanted to sell different kinds of merchandise, to open stores in cities and suburbs, to start a catalog, and to end J. C. Penney's cash-only policy. Batten saw danger for J. C.

Penney and wanted to alert upper management.

But Batten faced problems. Who would believe there was trouble ahead? J. C. Penney had just rung up $1 billion in annual sales, a record. In addition, Batten bothered people. And that made it difficult for him to win people over. Colleagues admitted Batten had abilities, but they didn't always like hearing what he had to say. One colleague said that Batten "walked a fine line between getting promoted and getting fired."[14]

Batten decided he had to tell J. C. Penney's Board of Directors about his concerns. He gathered his courage and put his career on the line. He gave the Board of Directors a 150-page memo, which said that the company was being passed by and that, without changes, it would fail. When J. C. Penney—the founder—heard Batten's suggested changes, he became sick. He gave his opposing views and left the meeting to go home. But the board was impressed. The members outvoted J. C. Penney and supported Batten's recommendations. Soon after, they made Batten president of J. C. Penney so he could implement the changes.

Two not-so-apparent aspects of this anecdote make what Batten did an especially good example of using courage at work. First, nothing forced him to act. No crisis brought matters to a head, compelling him to take the risk he did. He took it upon himself to do what he thought was right. Second, Batten resisted the urge to settle. His decision to speak up carried considerable risk, and there must have been a temptation to water down his recommendations or simply hint that J. C. Penny should consider rethinking its policies. Batten didn't take the easy way out, nor did he opt for doing something that might be just good enough. Instead, he took a risk and did the right thing all the way. He used the virtue of courage.

How to Use Courage

Courage requires you to ask yourself this question when facing a situation that involves some risk: "What is the right thing to do?" Prudence (or sometimes another virtue) will show you the answer. Then, courage enables you to do it.

But what if you're reluctant to act? Ask yourself, "Why don't I want to do the right thing?" Is your reluctance driven by fear? (Keep in mind that fear can wear many disguises and can cause rationalizations. Use your reason to see through them.) If fear is the problem, your will becomes crucial. All virtues need you to exercise your will. But courage, especially, is the virtue that asks you to call upon your will to do the right thing in spite of fear. To use courage, as the advertising slogan says, you "just do it."

Sometimes doing the right thing requires making a change, as in Batten's recommendations. But perseverance—sticking to your guns—can also be courageous. Perseverance asks you to remain faithful to what you're doing in the face of setbacks, changing conditions, and pressure for change, if your reason tells you not to change course. It requires courage to stay on course in the face of pressure to change. Prudence is especially helpful when you are deciding if you should change course. For example, prudence can help you determine if a change would be a smart compromise or a cowardly settling.

Courage On the Job...and Off

You use the virtue of courage largely through small actions. These build the habit you can call on when more is at stake—at work or outside of work. Here are some examples:

- When you've made a mistake, come forward and admit it. Don't hide and hope nobody notices.

- When asked for your thoughts, say what you really think—nicely, and be honest.

- If someone is doing something that doesn't seem right, ask him or her about it—even if it's your manager.

- When given several options, resist the urge to play it safe or split the difference, if that isn't really the right thing to do.

- If you're doing something that hasn't yet worked out, don't give up. If you still think it's the right thing to do, stay the course, even when it gets lonely and difficult.

When facing uncertainty, people look for a leader, and courage goes a long way to making you that leader. Using the virtue of courage gives you a history of doing what you should and a moral authority that has been earned and can't be taken away. People will admire you and your courage, making you a role model for your coworkers, friends, and family.

Not Using Courage— The Self-Destructive Habits

If courage were easy, more people would use it. But emotions—especially the fear of losing something you value—are strong; they make it easy to rationalize not doing the right thing. But taking that path comes at a cost; over time, you'll make self-destructive behaviors a habit, instead of courage. The virtue of courage guides you away from:

Cowardice. You know what the right thing to do is, but you don't do it. You let fear take over. You surrender to fear because you'd rather play it safe. The fear of loss is driving you. Paradoxically, for some people, the more they have, the harder it is for them to be courageous; they choose to be cowardly rather than risk the loss of some of what they have.

Recklessness. Reason doesn't drive you; rather,

impulse and emotion do. You act without even thinking about what the right thing to do is. And you don't consider the severity of the possible loss or its chances of happening before you leap into action. You're unpredictable and become undependable.

Courage Wins People Over

Courage, like all the virtues, involves a choice. You choose to be courageous, or you choose to be cowardly or reckless. When you choose to put fear in the driver's seat, you do so because you're focusing largely on yourself and what you have to lose. The virtues stop you from focusing on yourself and from acting for self-centered reasons. Being self-centered won't improve your relationships, your life at work, or your life outside of work, but choosing to be courageous will.

People will respect you for using courage, but you'll also have greater self-respect. Self-respect brings you confidence and a healthy pride that makes life more enjoyable. And it leads to an ability to take smart risks. Success in life—your professional life and your personal life—requires taking smart risks. Courage enables you to take the risks necessary to thrive.

Courage Leads to Other Great Habits

For Aristotle, courage was the essential virtue. He believed you had to have courage to be able to practice other virtues. Like courage, other habits enable you to do what is right under difficult circumstances. Using the virtue of courage is the best way to develop these habits. Some of these habits are as follows:

✓ Patience   ✓ Forbearance

✓ Caution   ✓ Commitment

"Self-discipline enables you to think first and act afterward."

Napoleon Hill,
American author

Self-Control, Which Leads to Maturity

"Impulsive, undependable, irresponsible." You don't see organizations advertising for these kinds of behaviors when they're hiring. But these are the traits you wind up with if you don't use the virtue of self-control; they're the traits of immature people. In contrast, mature people are ready for responsibility, for success at work, and for leadership at home and at work.

Self-control is fundamental. It helps you apply yourself and develop your talents so you can be successful. According to Peter Drucker—the legendary thought leader and management consultant—to be successful, it's more important to learn how to manage yourself than to learn how to manage others.

And self-control makes it easier to use all the other virtues. Once you use self-control to put a leash on your impulses, the other virtues require less effort and less will power, and they become your operating habits more easily.

When Do You Use Self-Control?

Self-control is about keeping your mind in charge of your actions. So you need self-control every time an impulse is gaining the upper hand—for example, when you know what you should do but don't want to do it, or when you're sick of work, or you're getting mad, frustrated, or bored. It's an extremely useful virtue. You certainly have used self-control, and you may use it often, but likely not often enough.

Working Definition of Self-Control

Self-control is using your reason and your will to moderate your impulses, desires, and emotions.

The key word is "moderate." Emotions aren't rational, and they're often dangerously intense. But your emotions and impulses are important; they contribute to your instinct, gut feeling, empathy, and drive. But you need to use emotions and impulses the right way, to be sure your whims and the passion *du jour* don't drive you. You'll find that proper balance with the virtue of self-control. It lets you use the positive side of emotions and desires, and it holds the negative side in check. With the virtue of self-control, you and your reason govern your emotions and impulses so that they don't govern you. Therefore, you're in charge, and you're free—free to act as you think best, to assume power, to do your duty, and to be responsible.

Self-control has another benefit that is often overlooked: lack of self-control diminishes you in the eyes of others. You don't earn much respect with tantrums, outbursts, or stinging insults, even if they feel good at the moment. They're childish and often unjust, and people know it.

Example of Self-Control at Work— Elliott White Springs

The big challenge for Elliott White Springs was controlling his impulses. Springs certainly led a colorful life, but he only started to soar as a person once he embraced self-control. The same is true for all of us.

Springs was the crown prince, and he acted like one. He was the only son of "the richest man in South Carolina"[15] and the heir to a textile fortune. Springs's father ran Springs Cotton Mills, one of the South's biggest textile companies. Springs went to Princeton, became a World War I fighter pilot and ace, and lived large. After the war, he wrote a book about the drinking and exploits of fighter pilots in France. But he continued his drinking and exploits back in the United States. In the 1920s, he toured speakeasies, drank heavily, chased women, and hosted all-night parties. He regularly visited friends with a "five-gallon jug of bourbon and a strange woman."[16] He worked in the family business, sort of. He was fired by his father for flying when he was supposed to be working. He was rehired, of course, but he quit several times, because he thought the cotton business was dull.

In 1931, Springs's father died, leaving Springs several million dollars and the textile business. Springs could sell off the mills and retire to a life of luxury. Up to now, he had avoided regular work. He was untrained and had no desire for the unexciting, regular life of a textile executive. He was undisciplined and unfocused—unfocused on textiles, at least.

But now Springs was in charge. He was in charge of the mills and responsible for the workers. And he chose to do what he hadn't felt like doing before—grow up. His daughter remembers, "It was like the closing of a door when my grandfather died and Daddy went to work."[17] Springs controlled himself. The flying stopped. The parties stopped.

And Springs went to work. The mills were heavily mortgaged and badly in need of new equipment. To save the company money, Springs slashed his own salary. He negotiated with creditors to stave off foreclosure on the mills, and he used all the money left to him by his father to rebuild the mills' equipment. Springs put a loom in his basement to try new ideas. He worked on Saturdays, visiting plants; he took care of every detail and never took it easy. Springs got the company through the Great Depression without laying off any workers, unlike his competitors.

He also offered his workers heavily subsidized housing and gave them generous benefits. And he started a foundation to give even more opportunities to the mill workers and their families. When Springs retired after twenty-eight years, his company had sales more than twenty times what they had been when he inherited the company, and he had turned it into an industrial giant.

Using the virtue of self-control, Springs learned to manage himself, and success followed.

How to Use Self-Control

The key to the virtue of self-control is to reason first, and then act.

This involves taking a moment to answer a quick question. When a strong feeling or impulse is pushing you to do something—or not to do something you should—pause (which breaks the feeling's momentum) and ask yourself, "Would surrendering to this impulse lead me to where I should go?" Your reason knows your goals, your circumstances, and your other considerations, and it will tell you the best way to handle your impulse.

Reason drives moderation. Taking this little pause to think through that question drains an impulse of much of its power and gives your will a chance to restrain the impulse, if necessary.

Impulse and emotion may seem hard to control. They seem to come out of nowhere. (And giving in to them doesn't control them; it only appeases them—they'll be back...stronger than ever.) But you can tame them with self-control. The more you use it, the easier it is to corral your wild feelings.

Self-Control On the Job...and Off

There are many opportunities to exercise the virtue

of self-control every day. For example, listen patiently to someone even though you know what that person is going to say, smile at the person you don't like, or wait until all others have served themselves before serving yourself. These are small actions, but all efforts that restrain your impulses make the virtue of self-control a habit and easier to use.

> Impulses are often self-centered.

The atmosphere at work—largely professional and focused, with people you don't know intimately—makes it easier to use self-control at work than at home. But even at work, challenges pop up that call for extra self-control. For example:

- Stress can easily cause people to lash out impulsively. Recognize when stress is building, and move to defuse the tension before keeping control of yourself becomes difficult.

- When someone says something unfair about you, don't retaliate.

- Put in the extra effort to take your work from "good enough" to "good job," even when you're tired or bored.

- If you see an outcome that will be to your advantage, push for it only if it's also a good outcome for others.

- If things aren't working out and you're getting frustrated, step back and put everything in perspective.

When you're in control of yourself, others see you as rock solid. You can be counted on through thick and thin. You'll still get elated or tired or fed up, just like everyone else, but you won't let those whims or moods control you. Procrastination and distraction are not problems for you. You and your reason are in charge. You rise to any occasion.

Not Using Self-Control— The Self-Destructive Habits

Emotion and spontaneity aren't bad—they shouldn't be banished from work or life. They can certainly be part of making a decision. But they can also be inappropriate and irrational. Using self-control won't make you emotionless, but it will prevent you from being dominated by emotions or being at their mercy. Without self-control, you can develop the following self-destructive habits:

Impulsiveness. When you're impulsive, your feelings are in charge. What you do depends entirely on what you feel like doing. Any emotion that grabs you dictates what you do or say. You become unpredictable and irresponsible. You give up easily and have a hard time doing your duty. You may, or may not, do what you have committed to do.

Coldness and Intolerance. Here, you ignore the human factors. You dismiss the contributions of emotion and feelings. Nonhuman considerations—the bottom line or efficiency, for example—dominate your approach to an excessive degree. You're overly rational, and, therefore, you have an undeveloped instinct and gut feeling. You lack a fighting spirit, the human touch, and understanding.

Self-Control Wins People Over

Impulses are often self-centered. Self-control, by moderating your impulses, leads you away from focusing on yourself and helps you put others first. And there is no better way to stand out, to earn the gratitude of others, to find true happiness, and to make the lives of others better than to put other people and their needs ahead of yourself—subject to reason, of course.

Self-Control Leads to Other Great Habits

Many wonderful, admirable habits logically flow from self-control, since they all moderate emotions. These habits become easier for you to put into practice once the virtue of self-control is a habit, and they all add to the respect and admiration others will have for you. The virtue of self-control paves the way for the following:

✓ Good temper ✓ Contentment

✓ Reliability ✓ Industry

✓ Frugality

"Humility leads to strength and not to weakness."

JOHN J. MCCLOY,
AMERICAN BANKER AND STATESMAN

Humility, Which Leads to Honesty with Yourself

Aristotle wrote that humility is knowing the truth about yourself. All of the virtues are based on the truth and reality. How can you be courageous, for example, without knowing the truth about the risks of a situation? With the virtue of humility, there's a difference. You're more concerned with the truth and the reality about yourself—what you're *really* like, what your talents really are and are not.

Now, you might not like the whole truth about yourself—nobody likes seeing their shortcomings—but you're truly better off seeing things as they are. You make better decisions, have better relationships, and are less anxious. Others know you're grounded and honest. The truth saves you from serious error at work and outside of work. Fantasy can be fun and good entertainment, but, to do your job well at work and at home, you're better off remembering Aristotle and working with the truth.

When Do You Use Humility?

Humility lets you see things as they really are. It is the lens through which you should look at yourself and your life. For example, whenever you're puffed up—feeling smarter than everyone else—or, conversely, depressed—feeling not as good as everyone else—humility can set you straight.

Working Definition of Humility

Humility is knowing the truth about yourself, about others, and about your life's circumstances, and then accepting those truths and their consequences, instead of basing your actions on something false.

Using humility keeps you in touch with reality about yourself and your life. Therefore, it leads to an honest life. For example, if you accept what's true about yourself, you won't fall into the trap of pretending to be something you're not and desperately trying to live up to it. Everyone has strengths and weaknesses. The humble see theirs, accept their strengths and the weaknesses they haven't gotten rid of yet, and go forward with them.

As with all the virtues, humility uses your reason and will. You use your reason to examine yourself and to figure out your strengths and weaknesses—and those of others. You use your will to accept them, especially when you would rather have other strengths or not have certain weaknesses.

There are myths about humility that fly in the face of knowing and accepting the truth about yourself. Being humble doesn't mean you have to put yourself down, submit meekly to others, or avoid saying anything good about yourself. And humility doesn't take away your drive or ambition. Rather, it can help you achieve your goals, because, if you know what you can do well, you can focus on those talents and develop them. The virtue of humility helped Alan Wurtzel achieve.

Example of Humility at Work— Alan Wurtzel

Alan Wurtzel, CEO of an appliance-store chain, was in a desperate situation. Reality for the company looked bad. So, he used humility—the truth about himself—to save his company.

Back in 1949, Alan Wurtzel's father was on vacation in Richmond, Virginia. While he was getting a haircut, the barber mentioned that the South's first television station was about to go on the air in Richmond. Wurtzel's father foresaw tremendous demand for television sets. He moved his family to Richmond and started a company called Wards to sell television sets.

> He used humility to save his company.

Wards grew. Expansion was rapid and a bit haphazard. Wards started selling appliances and then stereo equipment. It bought appliance stores across the country, some of which also sold furniture and tires. It sold via mail order, in department stores, and in specialty stores. It all worked…for a while.

In the early 1970s, a bad economy, rapid expansion, and acquisitions unrelated to its core business caught up with Wards. The situation was dire. Wards was losing millions of dollars a year and had huge debts that put it on the verge of bankruptcy. This was the moment when Alan Wurtzel, the son of the founder, was named

Wards's CEO.

People were anxious about his plans. When asked about how he was going to turn Wards around, Wurtzel had a humble, truthful answer: I don't know. The CEO didn't know what to do to fix Wards. That was the reality, and he accepted it. He didn't pretend anything else was true.

But Wurtzel did know where to get the answer. He tapped the strengths of others. He knew his board members and executive team knew more about Wards, the market, and appliances than he did. To figure out what to do, Wurtzel started asking them questions. He started with his board members; then he asked his executive team. He pushed, probed, and prodded until, using the superior knowledge and ideas of others, he knew what to do.

Wurtzel decided to close some Wards stores. He then put half the company's net worth into an experimental store that the executives and board members thought customers would like—a huge warehouse-style store called Wards Loading Dock. It was the first consumer electronics superstore, and it sold thousands of products. It was a big success. Wurtzel then closed more stores and converted others into the Wards Loading Dock format. Wurtzel's restyled stores continued to prosper, and, by 2007, they had 46,000 employees and annual sales of over $12 billion.

The virtue of humility has a wonderful effect on your

life in many ways, including an unexpected one this anecdote illustrates: it lets you see the strengths of others and ask them for help. Wurtzel saw that other people knew more about electronics retailing than he did. He knew he had different strengths, so he had the confidence to ask for help. If you're humble, you can use the skills of others to compensate for your weaknesses. And this makes you much more effective at work.

How to Use Humility

Humility gets you to accept the truth about yourself, about others, and about life. It's easy to blind yourself to what is true because of ego, self-interest, old ways of thinking, or strongly held assumptions that are really self-serving or untrue. For many people, the big stumbling block to humility is false or inaccurate assumptions that are fixed and determine how they see themselves and the world. For example, some people think of themselves as more talented or knowledgeable than they really are. Your reason moves you beyond these obstacles to find the truth—that is, to find reality.

To get your reason to guide you, look at your situation as an outsider would. Ask yourself, "What would an objective observer say are my strengths in this situation? What would the observer say are my limitations

> Your humility will have a tremendous effect on other people.

in this situation? What assumptions have gone into my thinking about this, and what would the observer say about those?" And finally, "Given the observer's opinions, what should I do?"

These questions can get humility to direct you on specific issues. But humility's real power and potential to lift you up come when humility is a point of view, a way of living that you always use. And these questions, when asked frequently, will get you there.

You'll see that the virtue of humility helps you face and accept reality in your life's circumstances. By doing so, it allows you to tackle life's problems head-on, taking action to make things better. For example, if life is running against you now, humility enables you to accept what's going on and to get to work improving the situation; others tend to complain, look for someone to blame, or remain stuck in misfortune.

Humility On the Job...and Off

Everybody has weaknesses. To compensate for them, it's common to project an image of omniscience and omni-competence. Humility breaks this. It gets you to see and accept your strengths and your weaknesses. Suddenly, you realize what's true for everybody—that you're only superior sometimes and that you should take a back seat at other times. Doing this in small ways every day builds humility into a habit. For example:

- When something comes up that you don't understand or that you need help with, ask for help.

- In your next discussion with others, listen closely, and if you see that others know more than you, defer to them.

- You have knowledge and skills that others don't. It's true. But that doesn't mean you're always right. Refrain from trying to impose your will in every situation.

- Someone has just told you what to do. You might not like being told what to do or even agree with that person, but accept it and do it this time, unless that person is clearly mistaken or is telling you to do something wrong.

- You have experience, knowledge, and judgment that others don't. Use these qualities to evaluate other people and their ideas—they might not be as good as they think. Then act on this.

- You can probably think of some people at work who make you feel unsure of yourself. Remember the truth: you have valuable talents and experience they don't. Show them.

When you're humble, you see things as they are. You don't puff yourself up or insist on getting your own way simply because it's your way. Instead, you live in reality, in the truth. People know they can trust your input, and what they see is what they get. When you have an expertise and a contribution to make, you let people know. You know your potential and your limits—and the limits of others. You respect others, but you aren't overly impressed by them.

Not Using Humility— The Self-Destructive Habits

It's human and tempting to project an image about yourself or to think of yourself as a certain kind of person—at times brilliant, very successful, superior or, at other times, helpless, lowly. But unless these images and thoughts are true, this tendency leads to self-destructive behaviors—very common self-destructive behaviors. It leads to false views about yourself and others—one too positive, the other too negative. Humility steers you away from:

False pride. Here, you think too highly of yourself and not highly enough of others. You often criticize others heavily and try to control them, making it impossible for you to lead effectively. You insist on doing everything your way. You dismiss the opinions of others, and you chafe when working with others and when doing your duty—you see them as beneath you and your talents. Your assessment of yourself is greater than the reality, and, unchecked, it can become delusional.

There is a good form of pride. Take pride in your accomplishments and talents. These are true, and seeing them for what they are empowers you and builds your confidence. False pride, on the other hand, poisons your relations with other people. It deflates them and chokes off communication. The interesting thing about false pride is that you're only fooling yourself. Other people see you as you really are—they see the truth. Maybe not at first, but they do over time.

Obsequiousness. Here, you don't think highly enough of yourself and your talents. This can lead you to downplay or to denigrate your talents and to see yourself as overly flawed. This makes it hard for you to take the initiative, to lead, or to contribute much. You stunt your growth as a person. You also see others as more talented than they really are and defer to them too much.

Humility Wins People Over

Your humility will have a tremendous effect on other people, making life at work and outside of work more spirited. Humility can improve your relationships with others, and bring about more open, more enjoyable, more fruitful interaction. Your coworkers, friends, and family want you to recognize and appreciate their strengths. Humility enables you to see their value and talents. Humility also helps you recognize when you need and must rely on the strengths of your coworkers, friends, and family. Being needed will make them feel valued, and feeling valued is powerful. When people know that they are valued—that someone respects them and sees they have something to contribute—they receive a tremendous psychological lift. They see more meaning in life, they flourish, and they're happy. And this ripples through their life and yours.

Humility Leads to Other Great Habits

Humility has a group of habits that flow from it. They all have knowing the truth about yourself as their foundation. These habits are yours when you make the virtue of humility a habit:

✓ Confidence   ✓ Obedience

✓ Sincerity   ✓ Modesty

✓ Cooperation

*"Hope arouses, as nothing else can arouse,
a passion for the possible."*

WILLIAM SLOANE COFFIN, AMERICAN CLERGYMAN
AND CHAPLAIN OF YALE UNIVERSITY

Hope, Which Leads to a Positive Approach and Motivation

Hope can certainly bring more joy and energy to life. Hope makes you positive, sunny, and more enjoyable to be around. And hope is a pleasant virtue to use. Some virtues need your will to push you to act in ways you may not look forward to. The results are definitely worth the effort, but it can be a challenge. Not so for hope. The virtue of hope gets you to act, and in a way you want to act anyway. And that's just the start of its wonderful effects.

But does hope belong at work? Is this virtue appropriate for the workplace? Hope is just a warm, fuzzy feeling, and wishful thinking—right? As commonly thought of, yes, but that is not the *virtue* of hope. The virtue of hope is a powerful tool that can help you greatly at work, while spreading contentment and excitement. It's not simply daydreams. A passion for possible, achievable goals, hope brings success to life at work and to life outside of work. Your use of the virtue of hope will inspire others; they will be drawn to your confidence and positive attitude.

When Do You Use Hope?

Why not use hope all the time? Hope focuses you on the great things that are within your grasp. You lead your life in a forward-looking way, reaching for and enjoying what you can achieve. You're better off looking at the world while filled with the virtue of hope. When you do so, life becomes more exciting, more fun, and more meaningful for you and everyone around you.

Working Definition of Hope

The virtue of hope is the desire for a good that can be attained and the motivation to work for it.

Some people long for a good that can't realistically be attained. That's not hope. True hope is built on reason, will, and reality: you know you really can achieve the good, and that motivates you. That's why real hope isn't fuzzy daydreams or wishful thinking. Rather, when hope is one of your habits, you're fully engaged with your work—convinced of a positive outcome and eager to do what it takes to get it. The virtue of hope asks you to work. Wishes, on the other hand, are easy, because they make no demands of you. Harvey Firestone, founder of Firestone Tire and Rubber Company, expressed this truth when he said, "I should not be exercising vision if I looked forward to a day when I should supply all the tires in the world. That would be just idle, profitless dreaming. In quite another class is thinking out ways and means to get a certain percentage of all the tires used."[18]

> The virtue of hope asks you to work.

Since hope relies on your will, you can choose to be

hopeful, or choose not to be hopeful. The virtue of hope is not a matter of personal disposition, as many people believe. Some people might naturally tend to be more optimistic or eager about the future, but everyone can choose to be hopeful and make it a habit.

Example of _Not_ Using Hope at Work — Ralph Burger

Ralph Burger rose from driving a horse-drawn cart for A&P grocery stores as a young man to A&P's presidency. But oddly, as A&P's president, Burger failed to use hope. Hope contains both the desire for something good and the willingness to take the actions necessary to reach that good. And that's where Burger went wrong. His goals were good and attainable, but he didn't do what was necessary to reach them.

In the 1950s, Ralph Burger was president of A&P, a retail giant. It was the world's largest grocery chain, employed 120,000 people, and had retail sales second only to those of General Motors. A&P helped invent modern grocery shopping in the United States by innovating to give customers what they wanted. It was started in 1859 when a former tanner bought tea from clipper ships and sold it directly to consumers, cutting out the middleman. This was the birth of A&P. Later A&P started to sell food, in addition to tea. Next, A&P pioneered the low-margin, high-volume business model for grocery stores. A&P later expanded the size of its stores and offered private-label goods.

Burger rose up on A&P's success and became friends with the men responsible for its retail dominance, the Hartfords. In 1950, Burger succeeded John Hartford as president of A&P. As president, Burger set two goals: he wanted to preserve A&P's profitability, and he wanted to preserve the reputation of his friends, the late Hartford brothers.

Unfortunately, as president, Burger acted as if A&P's success was assured. He "continued to operate the way he thought the [Hartford] brothers wanted him to—loyally retaining and promoting old A&P hands."[19] Before making decisions, he would ask, "What would Mr. Hartford do?"[20] And he adopted a motto, "You can't argue with a hundred years of success."[21] As a consequence of his management, new ideas were squelched, and innovation was stifled.

> Without hope you can easily turn negative or sour—but that is not the worst of it.

At the same time, grocery retailing was changing. Customers wanted even larger stores with more choices, including more nonfood items. Competitors responded, but Burger kept A&P stores the same old size. After all, the old ways had produced great profits and had made the Hartfords legends. Why wouldn't they continue to do so and enable Burger to achieve his goals? But

A&P's prices and stores were no longer what customers wanted; market share and profits began to slip. Burger refused to change, even after it became clear his goals couldn't be reached without change. Eventually, A&P had to pull out of several large markets. It was surpassed as America's biggest grocery chain, and, in 1979, it was sold to a German company. Burger had relied on A&P's past success, and he failed to do what was necessary to attain his goals.

How to Use Hope

Hope often pops up spontaneously, ready to use, but wishful thinking and daydreams can also pop up spontaneously. To determine if your excitement truly derives from the virtue of hope, ask yourself, "Is the good I am excited about realistic?" If it is ask yourself, "What can I do to bring it about?" If the good isn't realistic, be careful; you're being pulled by something other than hope.

Since hope is a virtue, it contains an act of the will. So it can be used even when it doesn't come up spontaneously, and it can be sustained beyond an initial burst of enthusiasm. To do this, whenever your enthusiasm or drive starts to fade, remember the positive goal you want by asking yourself, "Why am I doing this work? What's the good I am reaching for?" Thinking about how wonderful it will be when that good comes about will spark—or re-spark—your motivation.

You'll find that using the virtue of hope helps you in

several unexpected ways:

- Hope pushes you to take the initiative. You're eager to act because the goal you want is achievable. Hope ends vacillation, paralysis, and the inability to get started due to fear of failure.

- Hope helps you separate real chances for success from imagined opportunities or dead ends. Hope uses reason more than emotion; therefore, any path to the good you want is thought out and real, not the result of a burst of emotion or self-deception.

- Hope is particularly helpful in a crisis—at work or in your personal life. You'll find using hope focuses you on a good, achievable outcome to the crisis and what you need to do to bring that about. It's the perfect antidote to the chaos, false starts, and wasted effort that many people experience in a crisis.

- Hope motivates others. When you use the virtue of hope, you have a clear, positive vision, and you are ready to act. And that motivates others to work and help you—they see you as a winner.

Hope On the Job...and Off

Hope doesn't have to be reserved for your big goals or desires. It does tremendous good for you and others when it's used and reinforced throughout the day. For example:

- When brainstorming about a problem at home or at work, keep everyone's attention on solutions, not on current difficulties or the reasons why some suggestions won't work.

- When trying to motivate others, emphasize the importance of the achievable results that will come from their work, instead of improbable, pie-in-the-sky outcomes.

- Tell people about the benefits of what you're doing, not the effort it takes.

- When asking people about their work, keep the focus on the good outcomes they want and be positive.

- If you're on a roll and things are going well, don't ease up, assuming that will continue. Remember to put in the effort that will give you the good results you want.

With hope as a habit, you focus on the great things you can do. You become optimistic, and this leads to action and accomplishment. You see the promise in every situation, which helps you contribute in a positive and constructive way. Your positive outlook prevents stumbles from draining you of energy and protects you from negative, self-defeating behavior. Your habitually positive and inspiring behavior will have a dramatic impact at work and on your family and friends.

Not Using Hope—
The Self-Destructive Habits

If you don't use the virtue of hope, you can easily turn negative or sour; but that's not the worst of it. You'll form self-destructive habits that can have serious consequences for your career and for your life outside of work. Hope keeps you from:

Despair. This is a conviction that no good outcome is possible. You face challenges convinced that your efforts will fail or won't produce anything good. Despair drains the energy out of you. Why try anything if a good outcome is impossible? Despair makes you passive and listless. And despair is contagious, so those around you become drained of energy and give up. Despair is self-fulfilling.

Presumption. With this flaw, you convince yourself the good you want is inevitable. You're so confident of a good outcome you don't do what's necessary to bring it about. You surrender the initiative and drive that can make it happen. You may do a little work for it, but not enough. Presumption can prevent the good you want from happening; this was likely the flaw that sunk Ralph Burger's goals at A&P.

Hope Wins People Over

By its very nature, the virtue of hope has wonderful characteristics that make you stand out, that make you a role model, and that attract others:

1. Hope is infectious, improving the mood and the atmosphere around you.

2. Hope is self-fulfilling. It focuses you on the positive and motivates you, so you're confident and action-oriented, which helps you reach your goals.

3. Hope turns your emotions and desires into tools for success. These are powerful drivers, and hope makes sure your excitement is realistic and ties action to it, helping you achieve.

4. Hope makes you solution-oriented because it focuses you on the positive and the achievable and because it makes you forward-looking, which draws others to you.

The virtue of hope is widely misunderstood. It goes far beyond a sunny feeling. Hope gives you a confidence and a can-do approach to life that brings success. And, of course, it adds fun and joy to your life and the lives of those around you.

Hope Leads to Other Great Habits

A number of attractive habits are related to hope. As the virtue of hope becomes a habit, you'll also be admired for these other habits, which are also built on a positive, realistic outlook:

✓ Cheerfulness   ✓ Trust

✓ Clarity   ✓ Peace of mind

Recap—What You Know Now

You now know what the virtues are, their power for positive, lasting change, and where they can be used. If you are ready to use them and soar in life, I invite you to read Chapter 6: The Program. Before you do, let's recap.

- The virtues have been helping people for millennia—helping people lead outstanding, admirable, joy-filled lives.

- Work is an ideal place to unlock the power of the virtues—to turn them into habits and enrich your whole life—including your career. You won't be alone in this effort.

- Compassion and justice change how you interact with others, strengthening your relationships and reputation.

- Prudence, courage, self-control, humility, and hope change what makes you act. Reason, your will, and noble intentions drive your behavior.

- Small, daily virtuous acts create your new habits as effectively as the dramatic acts presented in the anecdotes.

- Failing to use the virtues is not consequence-free; you'll form self-destructive habits that undercut your work for a better life and make it harder to use the virtues when you decide to do so.

The choice is yours. On the side of using the virtues, you have the collective wisdom of some of history's geniuses, from Aristotle to St. Thomas Aquinas to Benjamin Franklin. You have the examples of those in your life whom you admire or whose actions you admire. Most important of all, the virtues are a gift prepared for you and offered to you by God. On the other side, think about it: is there anything more compelling or ennobling than the virtues?

The next chapter presents the Program, a straightforward, quick approach that will help you unlock the power of the virtues step-by-step. The virtues you tend to use now you'll use more often, and you'll make new habits out of the virtues you don't use yet. Once you choose which of the virtues to focus on first, the Program starts you on your way, and you'll start reaping its rewards.

6.

The Program: Making the Virtues Stick

The Program shows you how to make the seven key virtues a core part of your life. And it teaches you how to use your time—both at work and outside of work—to unlock the power of the virtues.

"But I am busy." Yes, you undoubtedly are, but the Program doesn't take much time. It has been designed to be effective, easy to do, and efficient. Watch the virtues become habits as you use the Program's four steps: Commit, Plan, Use, and Review.

One Virtue at a Time

When you're ready to start the Program, pick just one of the seven key virtues as your focus. Maybe you know which virtue you would like to target—perhaps someone has "suggested" one for you. If you don't know which virtue to pick, reread the definitions of the seven virtues, or think about how each virtue will affect how people look upon you, or think about the self-destructive habits each virtue will save you from. Then, simply select the virtue that appeals to you.

It doesn't really matter where you start, because the virtues reinforce each other: using any virtue strengthens your reason and will and makes you more aware of other people and their needs. This makes it easier to use all the other virtues; for example, focusing on justice also makes it easier for you to be more compassionate. And once you start using your reason and will, it isn't difficult to keep using them—like muscle memory, they become second nature.

> The Program doesn't take much time.

But the first step is for you to consciously decide, "Yes, I want that virtue."

Step 1: Commit

Commitment is the key to any achievement. When you're committed, you're willing to put in the effort needed to produce results. This explains why some people stick to their diet, improve their golf game, or become outstanding in their field and others don't. Commitment produces results long after your initial enthusiasm or a project's novelty has faded. Commitment makes all the difference. It gets you to rise above bad habits, comfort, and inertia to reach your goal. You can't change without commitment, and nobody can commit for you.

Your goal in this step is to Commit to using the virtue you selected.

Committing is not complicated. You make up your mind—set your will—to do or not to do something. (The other steps in the Program help you carry out your commitment.) But how do you know when you've successfully committed? The answer: when you consistently, voluntarily give up something you value to get something else, now or in the future. The Program asks you to give up some of your current habits for a better, happier, and more impressive you.

Tips to Strengthen Your Commitment

Use whichever work for you:

1. Think about the kind of person you are and the

kind of person you want to be. Be honest. How will this virtue make you the person you want to be? How will it affect your life? Try to be specific in your thoughts; the more concrete the results you expect, the easier it will be to commit. Then write down these thoughts—they're why you want to use this virtue.

2. Remember that when you aren't using the virtue you chose, your behavior isn't staying the same—it's getting worse. Self-destructive habits are forming. Which self-destructive habits are forming now? Is that what you want? Write down what those self-destructive habits will do to you, your loved ones, and your life when they get worse.

You can't change without commitment.

3. Look around you. Is there someone you admire? Write down how the virtue you're focusing on will make you more like that person. Look again. Is there someone you don't admire, whose character you don't respect? Write down how this virtue will make you less like that person.

4. Don't go it alone. You might find it helpful to get someone else involved in your virtue project. This can help keep you on track. There are several ways to do this: team up with someone else who wants

to use the virtues more; tell someone what you're doing, and arrange to keep that person posted on your progress; grow in this virtue for someone else—doing this for someone else makes it harder to quit.

5. Commit to doing the Program for a short time, perhaps two or three weeks, if the idea of a long commitment bothers you. But really do it for those two or three weeks. When this time is up, if you see this virtue emerging, why not commit for another couple of weeks?

Commitment carries you to the next step, which turns your determination to be a consistent user of this virtue into a Plan that produces results. Your Plan maps out the road to change. Peter Drucker said, "Unless commitment is made, there are only promises...but no plans." The next step in the Program is to Plan.

Step 2: Plan

The Plan is the link between your intentions (that is, your commitment) and your actions. And it is crucial to unlocking the power of the virtues. Life is busy and full of distractions, and, without a well-thought-out Plan, you can easily forget about the virtue you want to target. The Plan also makes you proactive. You've committed to turning this virtue into a habit, and rather than waiting passively to see if a chance to use the virtue turns up, the Plan gets you to think about what you can do to make sure you use the virtue. Finally, the Plan greatly increases the likelihood that you'll succeed, that the virtue you've selected will become a habit, and that the beauty of life with the virtues will be yours.

Your goal in this step is to make an effective Plan you can carry out today to use your chosen virtue.

To make an effective Plan, think through how you'll use your chosen virtue *today*. Go over the "Working Definition" and "How to Use" sections of the virtue you want to work on and think about what your day will be like. What will come up that will give you a chance to use this virtue? What opportunities can you create, or take advantage of, to use your virtue? Can you put some of the ideas in your virtue's "On the Job…and Off" section into your Plan? Small uses of the virtue count—no need to plan dramatic deeds.

Tips to Sharpen Your Plan

Use whichever work for you:

1. Take the virtue you have chosen and envision very specifically how you'll use it today. Do this every day before you get to work. Use your virtue's "Working Definition," "How to Use" and "On the Job…and Off" sections to guide you. Where will you be? What will the circumstances be? What will prompt you? The more specific your Plan, the greater the odds it will succeed.

2. Review the "Working Definition" and the "How to Use" sections for the virtue you've selected. The more familiar you are with the virtue and how to put it into action, the more likely you are to recognize the opportunities to use it that are hidden in everyday events.

3. Identify in advance the triggers—people, words, circumstances—that can help you remember to use your Plan. For example, if a certain person will benefit from the virtue you're working on, seeing that person can trigger you to use it.

> The Plan makes you proactive.

4. Anticipate the obstacles to using this virtue that come up at work, or that you put up, and plan a way around those obstacles. For example, suppose

you're getting pressure from a colleague to make a decision, pressure that may cause you to act impulsively rather than prudently. Plan a response that will satisfy the colleague, until you've had a chance to use prudence's three-step framework to make the best decision.

5. Go over yesterday's activities in your mind. When did opportunities to use this virtue come up? Or, looking at it from another angle, when did you feel a tug away from this virtue and toward a self-destructive habit? There is a good chance that something similar will arise today. Think through how to handle it.

Your focused, well-thought-out daily Plan puts you on the threshold of making this virtue a habit. The Plan helps you make the transition to the next, essential step. With the third step, the virtue comes out of the abstract and starts to have an impact on you and others: this next step is Use.

Step 3: Use

Now it's time for execution. The virtues become habits through repetition. Once you start Using, your new, virtuous actions start to replace your old, less virtuous ones. Your new behaviors muscle aside your old, increasingly self-destructive habits and build new habits that will make people admire and emulate you.

Your goal in this step is to Use the virtue today.

Using your virtue is largely a matter of seeing the opportunities (your Plan helps here) and of your will. But a significant obstacle to Using the virtue is simply forgetting to do so. Your detailed Plan helps, but it's still possible to forget the Plan, while concentrating on what is in front of you. To make sure you Use the virtue, set a deadline by which you'll Use it. Deadlines focus attention and move other matters and distractions to the side. Try setting a fixed deadline—for example, Use the virtue by noon or by lunch. Or consider setting a flexible deadline—"I will use prudence the first time I have to make a decision," or, "Today, I will help someone the first time I am asked."

> Now is the time for execution.

Tips to Help You Use

Use whichever work for you:

1. Keep your intended virtue in the front of your mind, because thoughts shape actions. Thinking about a virtue makes you less likely to forget it and more likely to find ways to Use it. So put up notes about it, look for examples of the virtue in the news or in other people, mention the virtue casually—anything to keep it in mind until you Use it.

2. Fix one or two times during the day (for example, by 11:00 a.m., or before your first appointment of the afternoon) to quickly go over your Plan and how you'll Use the virtue.

3. Prepare for chances to Use the virtue that you hadn't planned that simply pop up during the day. Think of the "Working Definition" or "How to Use" sections of your chosen virtue several times during the day so that you'll see requests, an assignment, or a meeting as opportunities to Use.

4. Use the virtue on matters that seem minor or unimportant. The key to Using is recognizing and grabbing the opportunity to Use. Simply using the virtue strengthens your reason and will and makes it easier for you to use the virtue the next time.

5. On the other hand, consider what would be lost to you and others if you had an opportunity to Use your virtue and you didn't Use it. There is a

cost when you don't Use. What benefits did you and others miss by your decision not to Use your virtue? What self-destructive behavior was just reinforced?

At this stage, congratulations are in order. You've Committed to using a virtue, Planned how to use it, and have started to Use it. Now, you probably would like this achievement to keep going; you want your success with the Program to develop momentum and to become easier. That's the role of the last, and easiest, step in the Program: Review.

Step 4: Review

The final step of the Program is easy, but crucial. It speeds adoption of the virtue you've chosen and brings its promise within reach. In this step, you Review daily your success—or your difficulty—in using the virtue you chose as a new habit.

The Review adds accountability to your Commitment to use this virtue; you know that you'll have to check and see if you carried out your Plan. And that adds just enough pressure to get you to Use your virtue. This accountability and light pressure are important because the only thing that will make this virtue a habit is using it consistently. The difficulty or drama of your actions isn't important; it's the consistent use of the virtue you selected that makes it a habit.

Your goal in this step is to Review today.

In the Review, at the end of the day, you compare your actions to your Plan. How well did you execute your Plan? The Review consists of going through these questions:

- Did I Use the virtue I Planned to Use?

- If not, what stopped me? What can be done about this? Would changing my Plan help? Would a different deadline help?

- If I used it, was it easier or harder to Use than I had

expected? If harder, what would make it easier?

- Did I see an opportunity to Use another virtue today? Did I take it? If not, why not?

By asking yourself these questions, you make yourself better at using your chosen virtue. You identify if, and when, using this virtue is hard for you, why it's hard, and how to make using it easier.

Tips to Help With Review

Use whichever work for you:

1. Review at the same time every day—for example, on your way home from work. Reviewing consistently will make it a habit.

> It's easy to overlook how much progress you've made.

2. Reward yourself if the Review shows that you did your virtue. The reward doesn't have to be big, but something pleasant. It celebrates a job well done and keeps you positive. Creating a new habit isn't always easy, and you're entitled to all kinds of encouragement. Be pleased with any progress.

3. Go over the reasons you're working on this virtue. Do this at least once a week, because this strengthens your Commitment. Focus on the benefits to you and to others from using this virtue more

often. If you're working on a virtue with someone else, check in with that person at least once a week for the same reason.

4. Be encouraged. It's easy to overlook how much progress you've made and to be disappointed by the opportunities you miss to Use your virtue. Every week, remember how inconsistently or how poorly you used this virtue before starting the Program. You'll be pleased with how far you've come.

The Program is time-efficient and will bring you results. But be patient. Nobody can change old habits or add new ones instantly. "Habit is [to be] coaxed downstairs a step at a time," Mark Twain wrote. Over time, you'll see that when you make progress with one virtue, it's suddenly easier to make progress with the other virtues; they're interconnected and reinforce each other. The more you use your reason and will and focus on others, the easier it is to keep doing it—like a muscle getting into shape. And it's the Program's four steps—Commit, Plan, Use and Review—that will help you make the changes you want.

A QUICK REVIEW:

Opening the Gift

Remember that you and God are on the same side. You want a happy, fulfilling life—a life that others can admire and imitate—and God wants that for you. In fact, God has given you the tools you need to have just such a life—the virtues. His gift to you needs to be opened and used. Strive to use the virtues in all your interactions, in all your decisions, and as the driver of all your actions. The more the virtues are used, the better the results are for you. That's why using the virtues while you work is so sensible.

Example of the Impact of the Virtues— Edward Stettinius & William Fairburn

The virtues belong at the center of all we do, including work. You and others benefit greatly from their use, as the compassion of Edward Stettinius and William Fairburn clearly shows.

Matches, a new product in the mid-nineteenth century, were becoming a big business. But all match manufacturers had a serious problem: they were poisoning their own workers. A primary ingredient of matches was white phosphorous, which is a powerful poison. The fumes given off by white phosphorous during the production of matches led to a condition called phosphorous necrosis or "phossy jaw." Phosphorous necrosis brought about a painful death, but first it caused workers' jaws to deteriorate, leaving them disfigured and able to eat and speak only with great difficulty.

> The virtues are a power for good.

In the early 1900s, Diamond Match Company was the biggest U.S. manufacturer of matches, but it was struggling. Edward Stettinius was hired and made president of Diamond to bring order to the company and restore profitability. William Fairburn was a naval architect, whose production skills caught the attention of Diamond Match's Board of Directors, and, in 1909, they hired Fairburn as Diamond's head of production.

Stettinius and Fairburn made the needs of Diamond's employees a priority; in other words, they used the virtue of compassion while they managed Diamond Match. They spent money to improve conditions for Diamond's workers through better cafeterias and free coffee. But, most important, they had engineers develop air conditioning and air cleaning mechanisms to improve the ventilation in Diamond's factories, which cut the level of noxious fumes and improved working conditions. But phosphorous necrosis remained a significant problem.

Diamond had a chemistry department, and Stettinius and Fairburn directed it to develop a nonpoisonous form of phosphorous. Under Fairburn's guidance, Diamond's chemists eventually succeeded. They created the safety match; the new chemical composition of the match head made a match that was safe to manufacture and safer to use.

But Stettinius' compassion was just getting started: he persuaded Diamond's Board of Directors to give Diamond's patent for the safety match to the public, which really meant to his competitors. Stettinius' compassion for his competitors' employees led him to give away Diamond's biggest competitive advantage. Furthermore, to speed up introduction of the new manufacturing process, Stettinius ordered Diamond's engineers and chemists to teach Diamond's competitors the new match-making process.

The press praised Diamond Match, calling it a public benefactor, and Diamond won awards for eliminating a significant occupational hazard. The safety match sparked an increase in match sales, and Diamond eventually controlled 90 percent of U.S. match production.

Stettinius received widespread acclaim; his integrity was praised in particular. His actions and integrity were crucial in the JP Morgan Company's decisions to hire Stettinius for an extremely powerful, sensitive position during World War I and to make him a partner in the firm. Fairburn was made president of Diamond Match in 1915. And he continued his compassion; Fairburn strove to make working conditions even better, and he found opportunities to raise wages at Diamond, even during the Great Depression.

The Gift and This Book

If you are perfect, you don't need this book to open the gift of the virtues, but most people aren't, and they need help using the virtues more frequently. The virtues are a power for good, so there are immense benefits from making the virtues even a slightly bigger part of your life. This book and the Program have been designed to help you—they help you open the gift. They explain what the gift is, when to use it, and how to use it:

What the Gift Is—The virtues. They have improved lives for millennia. They draw on your greatest capabilities as a human. The virtues develop the good within you: they bring it to the surface, make it something you use and something that is noticed.

When to Use the Gift—The gift can be used all the time—anywhere you are, at home or at play. But one particularly smart place to give it a try is at work. How you act at work goes a long way to setting your life's habits. You spend a lot of time there, and work habits bleed over to your life outside of work—which is the more important part of your life. So use the virtues on the job. Watch their impact on others and on how you feel about yourself. Once you're committed to the virtues, you start to soar at work and in life and to prevent self-destructive behaviors from pulling you down.

How to Use the Gift—The Program makes the virtues your new habits about as easily as possible. When you choose to put the Program into practice, your older, less good habits, and all their self-destructive effects are replaced. You don't have to struggle to eliminate them; the good ones dispose of them for you. And the power and the promise of the virtuous life are yours.

When you open the gift and use it, you become an admired person. You're valued for your judgment and consulted because you have an open, fair and realistic mind. You're in command of yourself. You lead others effectively because they respect you. You care about others and do what needs to be done. You see life's possibilities and promise. The gift makes you a great worker, the kind that gets rewarded. It makes you a great friend, spouse, and parent. It makes you a great person, a person with a rich life who enriches the lives of others—at work and outside of work. It makes you soar.

Endnotes

Good Things Happen When the Virtues Are Habits
1 Jonathan T.F. Weisberg, "Are CEOs today's heroes?," *Yale Insights,*
January 1, 2011, 57.

"One factor we called personal dynamism. It isn't charisma so much as
the backslapping, gregarious kind of salesmanship dimension...A second cluster of factors has to do with recognition of others, concern for
the welfare of employees, knowing who's around you. It goes beyond
interpersonal emotional intelligence to a sort of collective empathy.
A third factor has to do with authenticity, and what came out on that
dimension was the moral model that they set and their credibility, the
proverbial walking of the talk. Then the fourth category has to do with
setting inspirational goals. It is stretching people, setting higher standards. The fifth and last one, which is an especially problematic one
in recent years, is what we called boldness—prudent risk-taking." The
second, third, fourth and fifth factors that Prof. Sonnenfeld identifies
tie directly into compassion, integrity (which is a product of using the
virtues consistently), hope and prudence.

2 Randall Beck and Jim Harter, "Why Great Managers Are So Rare,"
Gallup, http://www.gallup.com/businessjournal/167975/why-great-
managers-rare.aspx (accessed June 1, 2017).

"Gallup finds that great managers have the following talents: They
motivate every single employee to take action and engage employees
with a compelling mission and vision. They have the assertiveness to
drive outcomes and the ability to overcome adversity and resistance.
They create a culture of clear accountability. They build relationships
that create trust, open dialogue, and full transparency. They make
decisions based on productivity, not politics." These talents come from
using the virtues of hope, courage, justice, compassion and prudence,
respectively.

3 Sharon Allen, "Leadership and Ethics," University of Notre Dame, Mendoza College of Business, http://mendoza.nd.edu (accessed January 29, 2009).

The Virtues
4 Michael B. Smith and Janet Loehrke, "Not Unplugged," *USA Today*, May 24, 2017.

5 "Many Employees Feel Compelled to Connect Outside of Work Hours," Ipsos Public Affairs, June 17, 2014.

What If You Don't Use the Virtues?
6 John Pepper, "What Really Matters: Services, Leadership, People and Values," University of Notre Dame, Mendoza College of Business, http://mendoza.nd.edu (accessed February 13, 2009).

Compassion, Which Leads to Kindness
7 Evan Carmichael, "Lesson 5 Invest Your Money in People," *EvanCarmichael,* http://www.evancarmichael.com/Famous-Entrepreneurs/3033/Lesson-5-Invest-Your-Money-in-People.html (accessed October 22, 2008).

8 Benjamin Hunnicutt, Kellogg's *Six-Hour Day* (Philadelphia: Temple University Press, 1996), 15.

9 Ibid., 16.

Justice, Which Leads to Fairness
10 Peter Elkind, "The Trouble with Steve Jobs," *Fortune*, http://fortune.com/2008/03/05/the-trouble-with-steve-jobs/ (accessed June 7, 2011).

11 Ibid., (accessed June 7, 2011).

12 Scott Raymond, "Steve Jobs: Apple's greatest legacy or its biggest obstacle?," *ZDNet,* http://www.zdnet.com/article/steve-jobs-apples-greatest-legacy-or-its-biggest-obstacle/ (accessed September 1,2011).

Prudence, Which Leads to Wisdom
13 Tom McGhee, "Anschutz's Ingenuity Flared in Deal with Firefighter, Studio," Business, *The Denver Post,* November 5, 2005.

Courage, Which Leads to Bravery
14 Kenneth T. Jackson and Karen Markoe, *The Scribner Encyclopedia of American Lives: 1997-1999* (Farmington Hills: Gale/Cengage Learning, 2001), 41.

Self-Control, Which Leads to Maturity
15 John Steele Gordon, "Redeeming Time," *American Heritage,* http://www.americanheritage.com/content/redeeming-time (accessed May 30, 2007).

16 Burke Davis, *War Bird: The Life and Times of Elliott White Springs* (Chapel Hill: University of North Carolina Press, 1987), 129.

17 Ibid., 131.

Hope, Which Leads to a Positive Approach and Motivation
18 Julie Fenster, *In the Words of Great Business Leaders* (New York: John Wiley & Sons, Inc., 2000), 242.

19 John N. Ingham, *Biographical Dictionary of American Business Leaders H-M* (Westport: Greenwood Press, 1983), 556.

20 J. Patrick Dobel, "Managerial Leadership and the Ethical Importance of Legacy," in *Public Ethics and Governance: Standards and Practices in Comparative Perspective* ed. Denis Saint-Martin and Fred Thompson (Boston: Elsevier JAI, 2006), 199.

21 George Wells, "John Maxwell: Today Matters," *documents.mx*, http://documents.mx/documents/maxwell-today-matters.html (accessed May 19, 2009).

About the Author

Alexander Cummings is a former marketing consultant. He advised some of the world's best-known corporations on branding, naming, marketing, and communications. He also worked with corporations to develop and to implement their corporate-values programs. In addition, Alexander served as a consultant to nonprofit organizations in the United States and Europe, strengthening their management and marketing. He has also taught on character and leadership. He received his MBA from Yale University and a BA in economics from Vanderbilt University. He is married and has two children. Alexander is available for speaking engagements.

Illustration: To Unlock the Power of the Virtues

Consistently Use One or More of the Virtues...

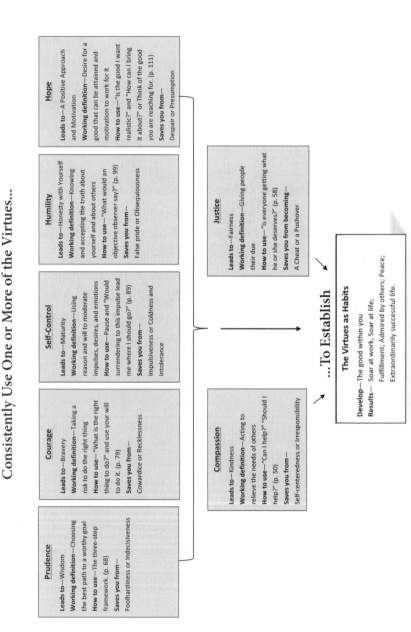

Prudence

Leads to—Wisdom

Working definition—Choosing the best path to a worthy goal

How to use—The three-step framework. (p. 68)

Saves you from—
Foolhardiness or Indecisiveness

Courage

Leads to—Bravery

Working definition—Taking a risk to do the right thing

How to use—"What is the right thing to do?" and use your will to do it. (p. 79)

Saves you from—
Cowardice or Recklessness

Self-Control

Leads to—Maturity

Working definition—Using reason and will to moderate impulses, desires, and emotions

How to use—Pause and "Would surrendering to this impulse lead me where I should go?" (p. 89)

Saves you from—
Impulsiveness or Coldness and intolerance

Humility

Leads to—Honesty with Yourself

Working definition—Knowing and accepting the truth about yourself and about others

How to use—"What would an objective observer say?" (p. 99)

Saves you from—
False pride or Obsequiousness

Hope

Leads to—A Positive Approach and Motivation

Working definition—Desire for a good that can be attained and motivation to work for it

How to use—"Is the good I want realistic?" and "How can I bring it about?" or Think of the good you are reaching for. (p. 111)

Saves you from—
Despair or Presumption

Compassion

Leads to—Kindness

Working definition—Acting to relieve the needs of others

How to use—"Can I help?" "Should I help?" (p. 50)

Saves you from—
Self-centeredness or Irresponsibility

Justice

Leads to—Fairness

Working definition—Giving people their due

How to use—"Is everyone getting what he or she deserves?" (p. 58)

Saves you from becoming—
A Cheat or a Pushover

...To Establish

The Virtues as Habits

Develop—The good within you

Results—Soar at work, Soar at life; Fulfillment; Admired by others; Peace; Extraordinarily successful life.

Visit virtueswork.com to print this Illustration.